Building Library Collections on Aging

Building Library Collections on Aging

A Selection Guide and Core List

Mary Jo Brazil

Santa Barbara, California
Oxford, England

Copyright © 1990 by Mary Jo Brazil

All rights reserved. No part of this publication may be reproduced, stored in a retrieval system, or transmitted, in any form or by any means, electronic, mechanical, photocopying, recording, or otherwise, except for the inclusion of brief quotations in a review, without prior permission in writing from the publishers.

Library of Congress Cataloging-in-Publication Data
Brazil, Mary Jo, 1935–
   Building library collections on aging : a selection guide and core list / Mary Jo Brazil.
     p. cm.
   Includes bibliographical references and index.
   1. Libraries—Special collections—Aging. 2. Aging—Bibliography—Methodology. 3. Gerontology—Bibliography. 4. Old age—Bibliography. 5. Aging—Bibliography. 6. Aged—Bibliography. I. Title.
   Z688.A58B7   1990   025.2'761267—dc20   90-42163

ISBN 0-87436-559-7 (alk. paper)

97 96 95 94 93 92 91 90   10 9 8 7 6 5 4 3 2 1

ABC-CLIO, Inc.
130 Cremona Drive, P.O. Box 1911
Santa Barbara, California 93116-1911

Clio Press Ltd.
55 St. Thomas' Street
Oxford, OX1 1JG, England

This book is Smyth-sewn and printed on acid-free paper ∞.
Manufactured in the United States of America

For my mother and grandmother

Contents

Preface, ix
Introduction, 3

The Collection, 7
Policy Statement, 7
Selection Criteria, 7
Building Collections, 8
Selection Aids, 9

The Core List, 21
General Reference Materials, 21
Aging, 29
Alcohol and Drug Abuse, 40
Alzheimer's Disease, Dementias, and Brain Disease, 42
Caregiving, 47
Death, Dying, and Hospice, 53
Economics and Insurance, 58
Education: Gerontology and Adult, 64
Elder Abuse, Crime Prevention, and Safety, 66
Employment, 68
Ethics and Legal Issues, 72
Geriatrics, 74
Health, 81
  Arthritis and Osteoporosis, 81
  Cancer, 83
  Cardiovascular Disease, 84
  Chronic Illness, 86

    Diabetes, 86
    Drugs, 88
    Incontinence, 89
    Menopause, 89
    Parkinson's Disease, 90
    Rehabilitation, 92
    Sensory Change, 92
Home Care, 95
Housing, Design, and Environment, 97
Intergenerational Relationships, 102
Long-Term Care, 107
Mental Health, 113
Minorities, 119
Public Policy, 122
Recreation and Leisure, 125
Resources and Human Services, 128
Retirement, 133
Sexuality, 136
Technology, 138
Wellness and Fitness, 141
Women, 149

Index, 155

Preface

This resource guide and core list are the result of my three years as director of a community aging resource center in a health care setting. My clients included staff of hospitals, agencies, businesses, colleges and universities, and the general public, the latter consisting primarily of seniors and their families and caregivers. This guide contains material I know will answer questions about such subjects as aging health, eldercare, retirement, adult education, and long-term care insurance—a wide variety of questions from a variety of people.

The content of this book is based on the assumption that those reading it have already decided they need material on aging; therefore, I do not cover methods of needs assessment.

The first part of the book, on building collections on aging, will be of particular help to nonlibrarians. I often help directors of senior centers and nursing homes, activity directors, teachers of older adults, nurses, leaders of senior support groups, and personnel from agencies serving seniors to create small collections of material on aging. They need information not only on what to buy but also on where and how to get it. This section tells how to get government documents, which publishers are strong in material on aging, and where to get free and inexpensive materials.

The second part of the book—a suggested core collection of approximately 400 items—constitutes a medium-size collection. It is arranged by subject and can be used by anyone, whether they need 10 items or 300. Those intending to start a collection on aging will be able to use the list for the development of a collection. The list will also serve those who want to expand an existing collection, such as the director of a store-front clinic who needs to add age-specific disease materials to an existing medical library. Even children's books are included, under "intergenerational" in the subject list.

Because I expect this book to be used by the general public, researchers, teachers of all grade levels, health professionals, professionals on aging, and librarians, the audience level is identified for each entry. To simplify budget planning and book ordering, I have included book prices and ISBNs (international standard book numbers) when available.

A number of classics in the field of gerontology have been included. Some of these are out of print (designated in the listing with the initials "OP"). Because it is still possible to get copies of these books in secondhand bookstores and because many libraries will find they already own them, I have included these titles in the list.

It is expected that new books and resources will eventually replace those recommended in this core collection. This does not mean, however, that for information to be relevant it must have been published within the current year. Older books on topics such as grief, love, how the body ages, and leisure activities for older adults have much to offer. This collection guide and core list is intended to be a practical, helpful handbook. I hope it will assist all those who have recognized the growth of the elderly population and the need for information about and for them.

Building Library
Collections on Aging

Introduction

Older adults are a diverse group. They include the newly retired who play golf and take expensive vacations, the frail patient in a nursing home, the pensioner who lives in a single room in an undesirable part of the city, and corporate executives. Because women typically outlive men, the majority of older adults are women.

This broad range of people does have one thing in common, however—their numbers are growing. The older population—persons 65 years or older—numbered 29.8 million in 1987. Their number has increased by 4.3 million or 17 percent since 1980, compared to an increase of 6 percent for the under-65 population.

It is generally agreed that this group can be divided into the young-old (ages 65–74), the middle-old (ages 75–84), and the old-old (ages 85 and over). Interestingly, it is this last group that is growing most rapidly. Due to the increase in life expectancy, the 85-plus group was 23 times larger in 1987 than in 1900, compared with the 65–74 age group, which was 8 times larger. According to the U.S. Bureau of the Census, by 2030 there will be about 66 million older persons, two and one-half times their number in 1980.

All these numbers add up to the fact that "graying of America" is more than just a catchy phrase. If for no better reason than the inevitability of changing demographics, librarians, social workers, clergy, and directors of clinics, senior centers, and nursing homes—all those who work with older adults—should consider developing a collection of information on aging and resources for this expanding population.

The older adult does not conform to a type. People in their sixties may be as different from those in their eighties as teenagers are from people in their thirties. Chronological age is not a good indicator of how healthy or vigorous a person is. Not only are old people not alike, but they are also growing more diverse every day. Their lifestyles are becoming more varied. We need to keep this in mind because, for statistical purposes, old age has been defined as age 65 or older, and we tend to fix on this number when thinking of older adult characteristics.

In taking the broad view of aging in order to provide useful information for this diverse, growing segment of the population, it should be recognized that there are four related but separate aspects to aging. The biological aspect deals with physical aging—the body's gradual loss of the ability to renew itself. The psychological aspect deals with perception, motor skills, intelligence, understanding, drives, and emotions. The third aspect—behavioral—deals with the aged person's attitudes, motives, social roles, personality, and adjustment to aging. Finally, the sociological aspect of aging deals with the society in which aging occurs—the health, income, work, and leisure of older people as these areas relate to their families, friends, and society in general.

These four aspects of aging—biological, psychological, behavioral, and sociological—are all interrelated in the lives of older people. In creating a resource collection on aging, we must build with this interdisciplinary nature in mind.

The realization that any collection of material must be multidisciplinary is helpful, too, in thinking about other groups of people who will use it: the middle-aged (ages 40–64); caregivers of the elderly, both family members and professionals; professionals on aging such as staff of health care and daycare facilities, senior centers, and mental health agencies; the general public; and students.

The following personal experiences illustrate information needs that can be filled by the resources of a collection on aging.

Patti is 58. She is a small, fair woman and asks whether she should be worried about osteoporosis.

Joe has recently learned he has a serious health problem. His doctor gave him some information, but he wants to know more.

Sally, who admits to being almost 70, worries that someone may break into her home and wants to know what she can do to prevent this from happening.

Tom, age 53, has recently lost his job with a computer firm. He needs to find work but doesn't know how to go about looking.

Jean's mother is coming from another state to live with her. Jean wants to find local activities for her mother and also wants to meet others who are caring for their parents.

It is difficult to imagine a library of any size that does not already have books or information that will be of interest or assistance to older adults or those who work with them. Typically, such resources have been added to the general adult collection as part of the ongoing process of collection development. When the needs of older adults coincide with those of, say, businesses, researchers, the disabled, or racial or ethnic minorities, materials have been added to library collections.

Recently, there has been widespread acknowledgment of the growing numbers of the elderly and a heightened interest in information about and for them. Publishers are including more titles designed especially for this group in their new lists. It is the task of anyone building a resource collection on aging to bring the scattered literature under control.

The Collection

Policy Statement

Before the selector begins to acquire any material on aging it is advisable to develop a policy statement for the proposed collection. The statement should include a description of the library user. It should also identify the subjects that will be included in the collection: Will it be a collection on the health aspects of aging? Will it encompass all of the field of social gerontology? Will it include listings of community resources? The policy statement should list the anticipated user needs that will be filled or satisfied by the subjects included in the collection. The statement must establish priorities and limitations, including such guidelines as a cut-off date (prior to which materials will not be purchased) or a commitment to acquire materials in a foreign language. The statement should include information about the format of the material to be acquired—books as well as tapes, recordings, videos, or films, if these audiovisual resources are to be considered.

Selection Criteria

In making purchasing decisions about specific items, the selector should consider the following criteria:

Purpose and Scope. The selector needs to establish the purpose for which the material was issued and to determine the level of coverage. Is it directed primarily to the older adult or to a general audience?

Subject Content. How well is the subject covered? Are staff and outside professional reviews favorable?

Comparison. How does this item compare with materials already in the collection? Does it add new information or does it supplement or duplicate existing information?

Level. Is the book popular in tone, or is it technical or scholarly? What is the reading level?

Authority of Author. What is known about the author? Is the author qualified to write on the subject?

Publisher. What is known about the publisher? What type of material is generally issued by the publisher? Is it a popular or scholarly organization? If an association or network published an item, what is known about the association/network and its objectives?

Timeliness. Is the information up-to-date? Does the author include recent developments or current thinking about the topic? If the work is a new edition, has the previous edition been rewritten and updated?

Cost. Cost will influence whether the selector acquires the book in paper or hardcover editions and whether a popular title is acquired in quantity. It may also influence whether particularly expensive items will be rejected.

Format. Each type of material must be considered in terms of quality for its format in such matters as binding, illustrations, quality of paper, size of type, or audio or visual reproduction.

Demand or User Need. Has the subject been requested? Will the material fill a stated user need? How much money can be allotted to this interest or need?[1]

Building Collections

The selector who wishes to develop or expand a collection of resources about older adults will need to keep the following points in mind:

1. Materials to answer information needs fall into many broad categories such as health, nutrition, mental health, or family relations. Each category has its own literature and, in many cases, selection guides to aid the selector.

2. Useful information is being published by associations and alternate presses. Generally, these materials do not appear in library review publications and are therefore more difficult to research, identify, and acquire.

3. A significant amount of publishing is taking place in selected areas like health, caregiving, and insurance. This level of activity is not always matched in other subject categories. There will, therefore, be an uneven development in the aging information collection.

Information comes in many formats. The selector must consider how the collection will be organized, shelved, promoted, and used, as well as judge its subject content. A videotape is useless to one who does not have a video recorder. A report written in technical language may not be understood by someone who reads at a tenth-grade level; that person may need a summary. Newsletters, pamphlets, and information sheets all add helpful information to the collection.

Of course, a collection does not have to be made up of books and other printed materials only. In addition, consider:

periodicals
newsletters and irregularly issued publications
pamphlets
government documents
recordings, either audiotapes or compact discs
videotapes
16mm films

Selection Aids

Common sources of information about new materials include:

1. Recommendations from staff and clientele
2. Personal research in bookstores and other locations
3. Book reviews in magazines and newspapers
4. Reviews in specialized library magazines such as *Publishers Weekly*, *Choice*, and *Library Journal*

Do not neglect number 4. Because aging weaves through so many subject areas, general review magazines often discuss some excellent titles. These special book review magazines are likely to be available at your local public library. Most of them also contain reviews of audiovisual and computer software materials.

Also helpful in locating materials, and available at the library, are *Forthcoming Books* and the *Cumulative Book Index*. *Publisher's Trade List Annual* gives information on a specific publisher's current list of books.

Information about magazines can be found in *Ulrich's International Periodicals Directory*. Reviews may also appear in general-interest magazines and newspapers such as *Time, Newsweek,* the *New York Times,* and *Vogue.*

Specialized Selection Aids and Sources

BOOK PUBLISHERS' CATALOGS

The following publishing houses publish extensively in the field of aging. Write and ask to be on their mailing list for publication announcements.

Haworth Press
10 Alice Street
Binghamton, NY 13904-1580
(607) 722-5857

Lexington Books
D. C. Heath and Company
125 Spring Street
Lexington, MA 02173
(800) 235-3565

Springer Publishing Co.
536 Broadway
New York, NY 10012
(212) 431-4370

Charles C Thomas, Publisher
2600 South First Street
Springfield, IL 62794-9265
(217) 789-8980

Using *Medical and Health Care Books and Serials in Print,* select publishers and ask to be placed on their mailing lists. Saunders and Wiley are standard medical publishers.

W. B. Saunders
West Washington Square
Philadelphia, PA 19105
(800) 782-4479

John Wiley and Sons
605 3rd Avenue
New York, NY 10158
(212) 850-6418

Ordering Books

The next step is to place orders for the books that have been selected. It is advisable to check first to see if they are still in print, which simply means that the publisher is still stocking the title. Check *Books in Print* or *Medical and Health Care Books and Serials in Print,* both of which will list prices of each item and confirm the publisher. If you cannot afford these reference books, check with area public or academic libraries to see if you can consult their copies.

After you've checked the item in *Books in Print* or *Medical and Health Care Books and Serials in Print,* there are several ways to order:

1. Direct from the publisher
2. From the local bookstore
3. From a wholesale book jobber

Each choice has advantages and disadvantages. The publisher is the most direct method. However, some publishers do not fill direct orders or have payment requirements that do not fit your organization's procedures. Publishers' addresses are listed in a single volume of *Books in Print* and in Volume 2 of *Medical and Health Care Books and Serials in Print* and in *Literary Marketplace,* also found at your local public library.

The local bookstore is also a good source. The disadvantages are that some specialized books may not be available and orders may take time to arrive.

The library wholesale book jobber is usually the quickest source for all but the most specialized books. Unfortunately, titles on aging are often in limited supply. Each jobber should have a list of publishers whose material they supply. It is best to send a list of needed books to the supplier for a price quotation with the understanding that if the books are not in stock, they do not fill the order. You can then order directly from the publisher.

An excellent guide to wholesalers is *Publishers, Distributors, and Wholesalers of the United States,* published by R. R. Bowker and available at your local library.

The following distributors all have limited stock of titles on aging:

Baker and Taylor
1515 Broadway
New York, NY 10036

30 Edison Way
Reno, NV 89502

Majors Scientific Books
1851 Diplomat
P.O. Box 81907
Dallas, TX 75381-9074

Matthews Books (medical only)
11559 Rock Island
Maryland Heights, MO 63043

Most institutions' purchasing policies prescribe limits within which the library must operate. If these can be bypassed, several distributors accept orders via computer, thus speeding the acquisitions process.

ASSOCIATIONS

The American Association of Retired Persons (AARP) is in a class by itself when it comes to publications. They lead the field for useful, inexpensive (or free) materials about aging. Because of their huge membership network, which receives news of publications through *Modern Maturity* magazine and monthly newsletters, any collection of aging resources will do well to have the AARP publications.

American Association of Retired Persons
1909 K Street, NW
Washington, DC 20049
(202) 872-4700

From the above address you can obtain lists of publications and audiovisual programs. For a list of AARP books, contact:

AARP Books
Scott, Foresman and Co.
1855 Miner Street
Des Plaines, IL 60016
(800) 238-2300

Also prolific in the field of publishing on aging is:

Selection Aids

National Council on the Aging (NCOA)
600 Maryland Avenue, SW, West Wing 100
Washington, DC 20024
(202) 479-1200
FAX: (202) 479-0735

Certain national associations devoted to serving special segments of the older adult population produce material that will enhance a resource collection at little or no cost.

Alzheimer's Disease and Related Disorders Association
70 East Lake Street, Suite 600
Chicago, IL 60601
(312) 853-3060
FAX: (312) 853-3660

American Association for International Aging
1511 K Street, NW, Suite 443
Washington, DC 20005
(202) 638-6815

American Association of Homes for the Aging
1129 20th Street, NW, Suite 400
Washington, DC 20036
(202) 269-5960

American Society on Aging
833 Market Street, Suite 512
San Francisco, CA 94103
(415) 543-2617
FAX: (415) 882-4280

Association for Gerontology in Higher Education
600 Maryland Avenue, SW, West Wing 204
Washington, DC 20024
(202) 484-7505

The Gerontological Association of America
1275 K Street, NW, Suite 350
Washington, DC 20005-4006
(202) 842-1275

National Association for Families Caring for Their Elders
1141 Loxford Terrace
Silver Spring, MD 20901
(301) 593-1621

National Association for Hispanic Elderly
Asociación Nacional Pro Personas Mayores
2727 West Sixth Street, Suite 270
Los Angeles, CA 90057
(213) 487-1922
FAX: (213) 385-3014

National Association for Home Care
519 C Street, NE
Washington, DC 20002
(202) 547-7424
FAX: (202) 547-3540

National Association of Area Agencies on Aging
600 Maryland Avenue, SW, West Wing 208
Washington, DC 20024
(202) 484-7520
FAX: (202) 944-5481

The National Caucus and Center on Black Aged
1424 K Street, NW, Suite 500
Washington, DC 20005
(202) 637-8400
FAX: (202) 347-0895

National Indian Council on Aging
P.O. Box 2088
Albuquerque, NM 87103
(505) 242-9505
FAX: (505) 242-8700

National Senior Citizen's Law Center
2025 M Street, NW, Suite 400
Washington, DC 20036
(202) 887-5280
FAX: (202) 785-6792

Older Women's League (OWL)
730 Eleventh Street, NW, Suite 300
Washington, DC 20001
(202) 783-6683

GOVERNMENT PUBLICATIONS

Government documents—sometimes neglected as a resource—supply a wealth of information about aging. Government agencies distribute some documents free; others are sold for a minimal cost.

State and local documents are the hardest to find. Your state library has documents from all agencies, and you should contact the Department on Aging, the Department of Health and Welfare, the Department of Housing, and any other state agencies that serve the elderly to be placed on the mailing list to receive their publications (or publication announcements). Local agencies rarely maintain mailing lists, and it is usually necessary to make an in-person visit to the Planning Department, the Housing Office, and other such agencies to pick up any publications they offer.

Although it's time consuming, writing to federal agencies, congressional committees, and state and local government agencies will yield valuable information for your collection.

To find out what the federal government is publishing, consult the *Monthly Catalog of Government Publications,* available both in printed form and online. Write to specific agencies to be placed on their mailing lists. The following federal offices associated with aging publish information that would enhance any collection of resources on aging:

Administration on Aging (AoA)
U.S. Department of Health and Human Services
330 Independence Avenue, SW, Room 4760
Washington, DC 20201
(202) 619-0724
FAX: (202) 245-6699

House Select Committee on Aging
300 New Jersey Avenue, SE, Room 712
Washington, DC 20515
(202) 226-3375
FAX: (202) 225-5505

National Institute for Mental Health
Center for Studies of Mental Health of the Aging
5600 Fishers Lane
Rockville, MD 20857
(301) 443-1185

National Institute on Aging (NIA)
9000 Rockville Pike
Building 31, Room 3C02
Bethesda, MD 20892
(301) 496-9265
FAX: (301) 496-2525

Senate Special Committee on Aging
United States Senate
SD G-31 Dirksen Building
Washington, DC 20510
(202) 224-5364
FAX: (202) 224-9926

Social Security Administration (SSA)
6401 Security Boulevard
Baltimore, MD 21235
(800) 234-5772

Ordering Government Publications

Federal documents for which there is a charge must be prepaid. Ordering from the government is facilitated by setting up a deposit account with the Superintendent of Documents. At the time the account is established, you specify how much money you want to place in the account. Thereafter, when you place an order, the amount of the order is deducted from the sum held in the account. To start an account, contact:

Superintendent of Documents
Government Printing Office
Washington, DC 20402
(202) 783-3238

Some government titles are available for purchase from:

Selection Aids

National Technical Information Service
United States Department of Commerce
Springfield, VA 22161
Order Desk: (703) 487-4780

DATABASE

Ageline
National Gerontology Resource Center
American Association of Retired Persons
1909 K Street, NW
Washington, DC 20049
(202) 872-4700

An automated database that can make the search for current information and publications more efficient, Ageline is the first online bibliographic database to focus exclusively on middle age and aging. It provides citations from journal articles, books, government documents, reports, chapters, dissertations, and conference papers. Ageline also offers descriptions of federally funded research projects on aging. It covers materials published since 1978, with selected coverage of earlier works.

The Ageline database can be accessed only through subscription to Bibliographic Retrieval Services (BRS). For subscription information, call BRS at (800) 468-0909.

AUDIOVISUAL MEDIA

A variety of audiovisual resources is available to enhance your collection on aging. The following two publications are excellent guides to audiovisual resources in the field of aging.

Audio-Visual Resources for Gerontological and Geriatric Education.
Annual. Pacific Geriatric Education Center, University of Southern California, 2250 Alcazar Street, CSC 110, Los Angeles, CA 90033.

The Great Circle of Life: A Resource Guide to Films and Videos on Aging. Robert Yahnke. National Health Publishing, 99 Painters Mill Road, Owings Mills, MD 21117.

As with book publishers, certain film distributors have an emphasis on subject matter on aging. The following is a selective list of distributors whose catalogs you will want to receive.

Churchill Films
662 North Robertson Boulevard
Los Angeles, CA 90069

Good Samaritan Hospital & Medical Center
Audio Visual Department
1015 N.W. 22nd Avenue
Portland, OR 97200

Terra Nova Films, Inc.
9848 South Winchester Avenue
Chicago, IL 60643

Another resource, Bi-Folkal Kits, are a unique programming option that should not be overlooked. They are multimedia, multisensory packages built around a particular theme or experience shared by all older adults. Each kit title begins with the word "Remembering" and each of the programs starts by doing just that. The programs come as slides or videotape or both and are accompanied by audiocassettes, booklets, activities, objects, and a program manual.

There are also mini-kits and slide sets for less elaborate programs. Current topics include music, farm days, the Depression, school days, automobiles, 1924, train rides, and county fairs, to name a few. The kits are appropriate for senior centers, retirement homes, community organizations, church groups, nursing homes, day centers, and families. They can be obtained from:

Bi-Folkal Productions
809 Williamson Street
Madison, WI 53703
(608) 251-2818

FREE AND INEXPENSIVE MATERIALS

Several organizations offer either free or inexpensive publications on aging. The following list consists of such organizations, and, in many cases, the titles of particularly good publications are included.

AARP (American Association of Retired Persons)
1909 K Street, NW
Washington, DC 20049

Write for a publication list and *Resources to Go.*

Selection Aids

Consumer Information Center
Pueblo, CO 81009

Request the *Consumer Information Catalog*. Included in this catalog of 200 federal publications are such titles as *Diet and the Elderly; Arthritis, Osteoporosis, Calcium and Estrogens;* and *Thrifty Meals for Two*.

Health Insurance Association of America
1850 K Street, NW
Washington, DC 20006

How To Use Private Health Insurance with Medicare is an especially good resource for older adults.

Krames Communications
312 90th Street
Daly City, CA 94015-1898

Information Catalog for Partners in Health is one of the publications offered by this group.

National Council on the Aging Publications List
600 Maryland Avenue, SW
Washington, DC 20024
(202) 479-1200

National Institute on Aging Publications List
Information Center/PL
P.O. Box 8057
Gaithersburg, MD 20898-8057
(301) 495-3455

National Institutes of Health
9000 Rockville Pike
Bethesda, MD 20892
(301) 496-5787

Q and A: Alzheimer's Disease is a good resource for those needing information about Alzheimer's disease.

Radio Shack Circulation Department
300 One Tandy Center
Fort Worth, TX 76102

Ask for *Selected Products for People with Special Needs*.

Sears, Roebuck and Co.
925 Homan Avenue
Chicago, IL 60607

To obtain a copy of the *Sears Specialog: Home Health Care,* write to the above address or phone your local Sears store. This is a catalog of useful products chosen for their special features that help those caring for someone at home.

SRx
Seniors Medication Education Program
1183 Market Street, Room 204
San Francisco, CA 94102

This organization publishes a newsletter and offers the free Personal Medication Record Keeping System.

U.S. Consumer Product Safety Commission
5401 Westbard Avenue
Bethesda, MD 20207
(301) 492-6580

Ask for the *Home Safety Checklist for Older Consumers.*

U.S. Health Care Financing Administration
Baltimore, MD 21207

The *Guide to Health Insurance for People with Medicare* is a particularly helpful resource.

Note

1. Adapted from the Free Library of Philadelphia, "Materials Selection Policy" (Philadelphia, 1976).

The Core List

General Reference Materials

BIBLIOGRAPHIES

Audio-Visual Resources for Gerontological and Geriatric Education. Los Angeles, CA: Pacific Geriatric Education Center, 1988–1989. 200p. $17. No ISBN.

This catalog contains a selection of audiovisuals for education, curriculum enhancement, health care, training, and general interest from more than 90 distributors. Each audiovisual is annotated and the listing gives length, release date, and information on where the material can be obtained. The publication is updated annually.

Balkema, John B. *Aging: A Guide to Resources.* Syracuse, NY: Neal-Shuman Publishers, 1983. 238p. $34.95. ISBN 0-915794-48-9.

Designed for workers in social gerontology, this annotated bibliography of books, journal articles, and government documents is arranged in nine sections. These include general aspects of aging, economics of aging, housing, health, institutionalized care, recreation, and education, and each has subsections detailing the type of material. Most of the entries were published in the 1970s.

Rubin, Rhea Joyce. *Of a Certain Age: A Guide to Contemporary Fiction Featuring Older Adults.* Santa Barbara, CA: ABC-CLIO, 1990. 308p. $39. ISBN 0-87436-547-3.

This annotated bibliography consists of 304 fiction titles containing realistic portrayals of older people. Each story or novel has central characters 55 years old or older and was first published in 1980 or later in

English. Each citation is annotated and includes information on alternative formats available (e.g., large print or audiocassette). Indexes allow the reader to find a specific novel or story by title, author, theme, genre, and alternative format. Librarians will find this work useful in book selection and in developing reading lists and library programs. Individuals will use this guide to find literature that illuminates tasks they are facing or to find popular reading in a favorite genre. This unusual and useful bibliography reflects the growing awareness of our aging society.

Yahnke, Robert. *The Great Circle of Life: A Resource Guide to Films and Videos on Aging.* Owings Mills, MD: National Health Publishing, 1988. 400p. $75. ISBN 0-932500-79-X.

Yahnke provides a manual that aids educators, health care providers, and media librarians in using some 80 films in situations ranging from inservice training to continuing education seminars. The manual is organized into six sections, such as "Portraits of Aging," "Intergenerational Relationships," and "Responses to Loss." While there is some duplication of films listed in other guides, the unique feature of this guide is that it summarizes every film by scenes and includes discussion questions and sample worksheets.

ENCYCLOPEDIAS AND HANDBOOKS

Maddox, George L., ed. *The Encyclopedia of Aging.* New York: Springer, 1986. 928p. $96. ISBN 0-8261-4840-9.

This major reference work provides concise, authoritative explanations for hundreds of terms and concepts relating to the life of the elderly and the aging process. The encyclopedia includes information on biomedical, psychological, and social topics as well as on the growing range of programs and services for the elderly provided by various professionals and community and government agencies. The level of presentation makes this volume readily accessible to students and professionals from many fields; it is particularly valuable to nonspecialists.

Schick, Frank L., ed. *Statistical Handbook on Aging Americans.* Phoenix, AZ: Oryx Press, 1986. 294p. $39.50. ISBN 0-89774-259-1.

This publication provides statistical data about the aged population in the United States. The data are the most recent available as of December 1985, except in a few cases where late 1970 data are given because no later figures could be obtained. The tables and charts were collected from over 120 publications, most of which were produced by the government. If readers need more data they should consult the references cited and the "Guide to Related Information Sources," which is arranged by agency or publisher. Although these statistics are available to anyone with access to the source documents, it is helpful to have them compiled in one book.

U.S. Senate Special Committee on Aging. *Aging America: Trends and Projections.* Washington, DC: Government Printing Office, 1989. 186p. Annual. Free from the committee.

This is the fourth edition of this book, which provides background information on the status of aging in the United States. The data presented provide a broad overview of the health, income, employment, housing, and social characteristics of today's older population. The charts and tables, gleaned from a variety of federal government sources, will provide timely and reliable information for individuals, families, business, government, and volunteer groups.

Wasserman, Paul, Barbara Koehler, and Yvonne Lev, eds. *Encyclopedia of Senior Citizens Information Sources.* Detroit, MI: Gale Research Company, 1987. 505p. $145. ISBN 0-8103-2192-0.

This encyclopedia was compiled as a quick and convenient survey of basic information sources on nearly 300 aging-related topics. The citations, supplemented by over 500 cross-references, include a wide range of subjects from health problems such as Alzheimer's disease and glaucoma to specific concerns of the aging such as retirement and terminal care. Under each heading are citations for both print and nonprint sources on the particular topic. Designed to be more practical than theoretical, this encyclopedia can be equally valuable to the elderly themselves and to their families, to students and practitioners in the field of gerontology, and to librarians.

DIRECTORIES

Data Resources in Gerontology: A Directory of Selected Information Vendors, Databases and Archives. Washington, DC: Gerontological Society of America, 1989. 28p. $2. No ISBN.

This directory describes over 30 bibliographic or reference databases covering congressional activities, government-sponsored research, grants, health, medicine, biology, education, housing, social sciences, and more. Several of the databases, including Ageline and the Clearinghouse on Abuse and Neglect of the Elderly, are devoted specifically to topics on aging. Others, including Social SciSearch and Medline, contain significant subsets of information dealing with gerontological issues.

Directory of Adult Day Care in America. Washington, DC: National Council on the Aging (NCOA), 1987. 200p. $19.95. No ISBN.

The directory was compiled from responses to a national survey of adult daycare centers conducted in 1986 by NCOA's Institute on Adult Day Care. The directory is indexed by state and by federal region and includes a listing of 847 centers serving nearly 30,000 functionally impaired adults. Each listing includes address, telephone number, director's name, parent organization, year established, hours and days open, program auspices, funding services, client charges, and services provided.

Directory of Nursing Homes. 3rd ed. Phoenix, AZ: Oryx Press, 1988. 1,280p. $195. ISBN 0-89774-414-4.

This state-by-state listing of facilities and their services includes admission requirements; activities; capacity; detailed information on full-time or part-time professional staff; and maternal, fraternal, or religious affiliations. For the first time, the third edition identifies those facilities owned by chains. This convenient directory eliminates the need to consult a variety of sources when trying to identify long-term care facilities.

An International Directory of Organizations in Aging. Washington, DC: American Association for International Aging, 1988. 350p. $39.95. No ISBN.

This directory presents information on associations, agencies, institutions, and organizations throughout the world that are concerned with the needs of the aging. A total of 136 countries are represented, listed alphabetically by world region. Organizations are arranged alphabetically within each country. All information was supplied by the organizations themselves. Included are a geographic index and a subject index to the organizations, which range from large, long-established groups to smaller organizations just beginning to build their programs. This directory will make it easier for researchers, policymakers, practitioners, and educators in aging to communicate with others with similar concerns.

Journals in Geriatrics and Gerontology: A Compendium for Authors. Los Angeles, CA: Pacific Geriatric Education Center, 1986. 74p. $8.50. No ISBN.

The Pacific Geriatric Education Center has assembled this information to facilitate educators' utilization of and publication in gerontological and geriatric journals. Sixty-five English-language journals are included, representing a variety of disciplines and areas of interest. Each citation includes subject area, publisher, editor, frequency of publication, and article length and style requirements. This publication is valuable for authors looking for the most appropriate journal for submission.

National Directory of Retirement Facilities. 2nd ed. Phoenix, AZ: Oryx Press, 1988. 888p. $175. ISBN 0-897740-450-0.

This new and updated edition lists, state-by-state, more than 18,000 retirement facilities. Entries are arranged alphabetically by state and city and provide facility name, address and telephone number, contact person, capacity, and facility type. Facilities are identified as those having personal/boarding care, congregate/semi-independent living, independent living, and life care. Hospital and public libraries will find this a handy resource for finding what specific care facilities are available.

1989–1990 Directory of State and Area Agencies on Aging. Washington, DC: National Association of Area Agencies on Aging, 1989. 156p. $30. No ISBN.

This directory will help families and professionals locate community-based services for older people. Names, addresses, and telephone numbers are given for the nation's 670 Area Agencies on Aging, each of which operates an information and referral system for its local area. The directory also lists resources for caregivers, key national organizations serving older people, and Indian Aging Agencies in the United States. As more and more families are caring for relatives in distant cities or states, this directory is an invaluable tool for connecting them to appropriate agencies and services.

1990 National Homecare and Hospice Directory. Washington, DC: National Association for Home Care, 1989. $200. ISSN 1047-5494.

Home care and hospice are rapidly growing areas of the U.S. health care system. The directory contains home-care providers, hospice organizations, and homemaker–home health aide service organizations listed by city and state. The listings include address and telephone number, name of director, description of services, and accepted payment sources (such as Medicare, Medicaid, and private insurance). The directory is a comprehensive guide for discharge planners, clinical directors, lawyers, health care consultants, and suppliers and vendors.

Nusberg, Charlotte, and Jay Sokolovsky, eds. *International Directory of Research and Researchers in Comparative Gerontology.* Washington, DC: International Federation on Ageing, 1987. 196p. $10. ISBN 0-910473-17-X.

This directory is the first detailed compilation of recent research projects in comparative gerontology in developing and developed nations. Covering the period from 1980 to 1987, the directory provides brief descriptions of over 150 studies and related papers and publications that cover the spectrum of aging research from biochemistry to the use of leisure time. The extensive index is keyed to topical areas and the nations/cultures studied. Individuals interested in comparative research on aging in particular countries or in specific racial or ethnic groups should find the directory invaluable for identifying related research and individuals engaged in it.

Peterson, David A., David Bergstone, and Jay Lobenstine, eds. *National Directory of Educational Programs in Gerontology.* 4th ed. Washington, DC: Association for Gerontology in Higher Education (AGHE), 1987. $45. 874p. ISSN 0148-4508.

This work is based on a national survey conducted by AGHE and the University of Southern California. Section 1 is a quick reference guide to gerontology instruction at 3,032 accredited institutions of higher education. Column listings provide information on the number of credit courses in gerontology/geriatrics and tell whether noncredit instruction or educational opportunities for older persons are available. Section 2 contains information on campuses that have indicated they offer at least four credit courses in gerontology. The full program listings include descriptions of the programs and their requirements, what credential is awarded, whom to contact, and financial aid available.

Raper, Ann Trueblood, and Anne C. Kalicki, eds. *National Continuing Care Directory: Retirement Communities with Nursing Care.* 2nd ed. Washington, DC: American Association of Retired Persons, 1988. 449p. $79.95. ISBN 0-673-24885-2.

Continuing care (also called lifecare) retirement communities are currently gaining popularity. Residents maintain an independent lifestyle knowing that nursing care is available onsite for any short- or long-term illness, and they know what their future health and living costs will be because these costs are set forth in the lifecare contract. For those who wish to explore this option, this directory will provide information needed to decide whether a facility meets their wants, needs, and budget. Facilities are listed by state with an index by metropolitan area and a special features index.

Resource Directory for Older People. Bethesda, MD: National Institute on Aging, 1989. 224p. $10. Stock No. 017-062-00143-0.

This directory contains the names, addresses, and telephone numbers of national organizations that offer health information, legal aid, self-help programs, educational opportunities, social services, consumer advice, or other assistance. Intended for older people and their families, students of aging, health professionals, librarians, providers of social services, and others who have a special interest in the field of aging. The organizations are listed alphabetically with a brief description outlining the purpose or mission of each, services provided, and publications available. A subject index helps direct the user to the appropriate resource.

U.S. Directory and Source Book on Aging. Silver Spring, MD: Business Publishers, 1989. 374p. $69.95. No ISBN.

Produced by the American Association for International Aging as a companion volume to the *International Directory of Organizations in Aging,* this directory is a survey of the U.S. organizations involved in the study of and planning for the aged. Arranged by state, it includes government agencies, private voluntary organizations, foundations, corporations, and publishers of works of interest to the community on aging. This publication will be of benefit to anyone who wants to know about the aging-oriented organizations in this country.

Weiss, David M., and Diane E. Mahlmann, eds. *National Guide to Funding in Aging.* 2nd ed. New York: Nassau County Department of Senior Citizen Affairs and the Foundation Center, 1989. $75. 280p. ISBN 0-87954-333-7.

All of the organizations listed in this guide are in the business of awarding grants and other assistance in the field of aging. The guide provides grant seekers and grant givers with data on the specific funding interests, requirements, and activities of private and corporate funders. The contents include descriptions of federal and state government funding programs, foundation funding sources, and voluntary organizations offering funding, technical assistance, or other support for programs in aging.

PERIODICAL INDEXES

Abstracts in Social Gerontology: Current Literature on Aging. Sage Publications, 2111 West Hillcrest Drive, Newbury Park, CA 91320. Quarterly. $48, individuals. $98, institutions. (Published in cooperation with the NCOA.)

Previously titled *Current Literature on Aging,* this is a guide to 250 selected recent books, journal articles, government publications, and fugitive material in social gerontology. Annotated citations are chiefly for material in the English language. In addition to the abstracts of recent literature, each issue contains an additional 250 bibliographical citations. The annotated items are arranged by subject with author and subject indexes.

American Statistics Index. Washington, DC: Congressional Information Service, 1973–.

Published monthly with quarterly and annual cumulations, this publication indexes and abstracts statistical material appearing in federal publications, including journals and congressional publications. This work is usually available in large public or academic libraries.

Index to Periodical Literature on Aging. Lorraine Publications, 9000 East Jefferson, Suite 5-7, Detroit, MI 48214. $150.

An index to core gerontology journals in the English language. It covers all journals—social gerontology to geriatrics. About 45 titles are fully indexed and about 35 more are selectively indexed.

Statistical Reference Index. Washington, DC: Congressional Information Service, 1980–.

This monthly publication indexes statistical material in over 2,600 non-federal U.S. publications, including selections from state governments, research organizations, and U.S. professional and trade associations. This publication is likely available in your local library.

Aging

BOOKS AND GOVERNMENT PUBLICATIONS

Achenbaum, Andrew W. *Old Age in the New Land.* Baltimore, MD: Johns Hopkins University Press, 1978. 237p. $32. ISBN 0-8018-2107-X.

This book details the role and status of the elderly in the United States since 1790. It describes the valuation in our culture's attitudes toward the elderly by reporting a historical perspective on the usefulness of old age, demographic patterns in the aged population, and the notion of old age as a national problem. Of interest to scholars and researchers, the book suggests that many factors in our history have contributed to the consistently poor status of the elderly since the eighteenth century.

Annual Review of Gerontology and Geriatrics. Annual. Price varies. Springer Publishing Co., 536 Broadway, New York, NY 10012.

This annual review first appeared in 1980 and until 1983 was divided into five content areas that were designed to organize significant issues and findings in both gerontology and geriatrics. In 1984 a decision was made to rotate the emphasis (in alternate years) between biomedical/clinical and psychosocial/behavioral specialties. Annual reviews in broadly based fields are difficult to plan and edit. This series has done very well in balancing topical material that will provide information to practitioners, clinical scholars, and researchers. It is particularly helpful in supplying information to those professional clinicians and researchers who may not have received an introduction into the fields that they currently occupy.

Atchley, Robert. *Social Forces and Aging: An Introduction to Social Gerontology.* 5th ed. Belmont, CA: Wadsworth, 1988. 527p. OP. ISBN 0-534-08790-6.

This standard text provides an interdisciplinary approach to the field of gerontology. Theoretical discussions are illustrated with research data. The fifth edition presents new material in the fields of social policy, security, age stratification, elderhostel, sleep, and home care. The chapter on the future has been significantly expanded, and there is an extensive bibliography.

Beauvoir, Simone de. *The Coming of Age.* New York: Warner, 1973. 880p. OP. ISBN 0-446-72182-4, paper.

While this book has been criticized for its depressing view of aging, its thesis, that treatment of the aging is "society's secret shame," is well documented. Using historical and present-day examples in varied societies, Beauvoir has written what is often considered the definitive study of the problems of growing old. A special complement to this encyclopedic work is a series of vignettes on famous historical figures in their old age.

Binstock, Robert H., and Linda K. George, eds. *Handbook of Aging and the Social Sciences.* 3rd ed. New York: Harcourt Brace, 1989. 454p. $65. ISBN 0-12-099190-X.

This handbook organizes, evaluates, and explains research data, concepts, theories, and issues in aging from the perspective of a variety of social sciences—anthropology, demography, economics, history, the humanities, law, political science, social policy analysis, social psychology, social work, and sociology. It includes primary reference sources and key issues for continuing research on aging. Considered the major collection of essays in social gerontology, it is most appropriate for use by researchers, professional practitioners, and students in the field of aging.

Botwinick, Jack. *Aging and Behavior.* 3rd ed. New York: Springer, 1984. 437p. $24.95. ISBN 0-8261-1443-1.

Botwinick's book has been a part of the gerontological literature since 1973, and this is the second revision. In 1973 the literature on aging was more limited, and the book was a sourcebook on behavior and aging. With the growth of the literature since then, this edition is more a survey than a sourcebook. It still remains a useful text and reference that adequately reflects the changes in knowledge and attitudes about aging and behavior that have occurred since the first edition; it would serve as a good text for university students.

Comfort, Alex. *A Good Age.* New York: Simon and Schuster, 1976. 224p. OP. ISBN 0-671-24233-4.

With vigor, directness, and humor, Alex Comfort exposes stereotypes of aging under various subjects from alcohol to wrinkles. Included are drawings and brief quotations from persons who have made important contributions during their lives. This positive book will help everyone, young and old, change their ideas about the limitations of old age.

Cowley, Malcolm. *The View from Eighty.* New York: Viking, 1980. 96p. $6.95. ISBN 0-670-74614-2.

Beginning as an award-winning article in *Life* magazine, "The View from Eighty" was greatly expanded to include further reflections and anecdotes and has become a classic among writings about the meaning of old age. Since the days of Cicero, writers have expressed what aging means to them, usually from the vantage point of their middle years. Malcolm Cowley reports from old age, with clarity and frankness, on his experiences—both the perils and pleasures—of aging.

Cox, Harold. *Later Life: The Realities of Aging.* Englewood Cliffs, NJ: Prentice-Hall, 1989. 2nd ed. 374p. $24.95. ISBN 0-13-524133-2.

This textbook reflects the interdisciplinary nature of gerontology and includes material from psychology, sociology, social work, anthropology, the biological sciences, medicine, and psychiatry in its discussions of the major trends and developments in the field. Written from a social science perspective, it presents an excellent overview of older Americans and the later phase of the life cycle.

Cunningham, Imogen. *After Ninety.* Seattle: University of Washington Press, 1977. 111p. $17.50. ISBN 0-295-95673-9.

This collection of photographs of old people, begun when the author was 92, provides a unique view of the condition of old age. The faces portray courage, wisdom, beauty, strength, dignity, despair, and loneliness—living symbols of aging without fear. Cunningham searched for the active aged, those who maintained an independent spirit—survivors. She herself worked steadily on the book from age 92 until her death in 1976, at age 94, seeking out subjects, photographing them, selecting the final photographs, and supervising the printing. Each of the lives symbolized in the portraits may be viewed as a triumphant victory over the pessimistic stereotype of aging.

Curtin, Sharon R. *Nobody Ever Died of Old Age.* Boston, MA: Little, Brown, 1972. 228p. $8.95; $4.95, paper. ISBN 0-316-16546-8.

Written with passion, anger, compassion, and sometimes humor, this is a provocative view of the aged. Through her personal involvement with the elderly, the author works to ensure that the old are considered a resource, not a burden. She demands that we regard old people as "human beings with a future as well as a past." This powerful indictment of how the elderly are treated in the United States will raise the consciousness and indignation of all who read it.

Developments in Aging. Annual. Free from the committee. U.S. Congress, Senate Special Committee on Aging, Dirksen Building G-33, Washington, DC 20510.

This annual report by the Senate Special Committee on Aging describes actions by the Congress, the administration, and the Senate committee that are significant to older U.S. citizens. It recommends program changes and notes future trends in aging. The report also reviews problems affecting the elderly in the areas of retirement income, low-income assistance, health, housing, and social services. The appendices contain summaries from individual federal agencies on legislation, funding, and other activities for all programs affecting the elderly. This is not an easy report to use because there is so much narrative to wade through and no index. There is a detailed table of contents, however, and plenty of useful information for those who persevere.

Dychtwald, Ken, and Joe Flowers. *Age Wave: The Challenges and Opportunities of an Aging America.* Los Angeles, CA: Jeremy P. Tarcher, 1989. 380p. $19.95. ISBN 0-87477-441-1.

In this book Dychtwald expands on his belief that the older generation is a tremendous national resource. *Age Wave* points out the challenges and opportunities of the aging population in the United States by explaining how the "senior boom" will affect each of us. Myths and perceptions of old age will be changed, those in their middle years will need to plan for an extended lifespan, and those over 65 will become financially and politically more influential. However, Dychtwald does not address the needs of those over 65 for whom the future will not be prosperous. Instead, *Age Wave* stresses the opportunities these demographic changes bring to marketing and advertising.

Erikson, Erik, Joan Erikson, and Helen Kirnick. *Vital Involvement in Old Age.* New York: Norton, 1986. 352p. $19.45; $10.70, paper. ISBN 0-393-02359-1; 0-393-30509-0, paper.

The authors present the life-historical data of 29 octogenarians and their children, collected over a period of 50 years in a Guidance Study done by the Institute of Human Development at the University of California–

Berkeley. In an attempt to understand the psychosocial process of vital involvement in later life, the book includes discussion of the experiences and interests of this group both in old age and earlier life. The final chapter covers trends in the aging of the U.S. population and suggests steps to ensure that the elderly can remain vitally involved.

Harris, Louis, and Associates, Inc. *Aging in the Eighties: America in Transition.* Washington, DC: National Council on the Aging, 1981. 169p. $18.50. No ISBN.

Attitudes toward aging and retirement first examined in 1974 in the published study *The Myth and Reality of Aging in America* are updated by interviews with almost 2,000 Americans age 65 or over and another 1,500 subjects ages 18 to 64. Also explored are intergenerational perceptions about Social Security, current health care, health insurance needs, employment, and education. Interview results are graphically presented using charts and summary paragraphs. This Harris poll is recommended for core collections as it is frequently cited in literature on aging.

———. *The Myth and Reality of Aging in America.* Washington, DC: National Council on the Aging, 1974. OP. No ISBN.

This survey was conducted by Louis Harris and Associates during June and July 1974. It contains the views of 4,254 respondents on the stereotypes and reality of aging. People ages 18 to 64 were asked about their perceptions of how people 65 or over felt about aging, and people 65 or over were asked how they actually felt. In addition, both groups were asked general questions on attitudes toward growing old, their interests, and demographic characteristics. This report has been updated in *Aging in the Eighties: America in Transition.*

Hessel, Dieter T., ed. *Maggie Kuhn on Aging.* Philadelphia, PA: Westminster Press, 1977. 140p. $3.95. ISBN 0-664-24146-8.

Maggie Kuhn, one of the most outspoken leaders of older Americans, convened the Gray Panthers in 1972 to urge the elderly to contribute to social change. In this dialog, she denounces the belief that experience is useless and focuses on the possibilities of older persons in church and community service. She details what individuals, young and old, and their churches can do in areas ranging from health and consumer protection to monitoring corporate power and responsibility. Maggie Kuhn is a pioneer and an original source, and collections for and about older adults should include her words and thoughts.

Neugarten, Bernice L., ed. *Middle Age and Aging: A Reader in Social Psychology*. Chicago, IL: University of Chicago Press, 1968. 596p. $20. ISBN 0-226-57382-6.

The emphasis in this volume is upon social and psychological adaptations as individuals move from middle age to old age. Major attention is given to age status and age/sex roles; psychological changes in the life cycle; attitudes toward health, work, retirement, and leisure; differences in cultural settings; and changing family roles. Although the textbook is addressed primarily to graduate students, it is a classic work that should be in any comprehensive books-on-aging collection.

An Orientation to the Older Americans Act. Rev. ed. Washington, DC: National Association of State Units on Aging, July 1985. $15. No ISBN.

The first edition of this book was highly praised for its comprehensiveness by practitioners, educators, and policymakers. In addition to covering all aspects of the Older Americans Act (OAA), it provides a detailed discussion of the policy systems on aging, of which the OAA is part; the essential issues pertaining to the federal legislative process; and the role of organizations on aging in influencing the goals of public policy. It includes an introduction to employment programs and related services that is particularly helpful to newcomers to the field of aging.

Palmore, Erdman, et al., eds. *Normal Aging: Reports from the Duke Longitudinal Studies. Vol. 1, 1955–1969* (published 1970); *Vol. 2, 1970–1973* (published 1974); *Vol. 3, 1975–1984* (published 1985). Durham, NC: Duke University Press. $37.50 ea. ISBN 0-8223-0238-1; 0-8223-0311-6; 0-8223-0624-7.

These volumes report the findings of the longitudinal study of aging conducted by Duke University beginning in 1954, including the original research articles and papers presented at professional meetings. The first interdisciplinary study of normal aging in the United States, the Duke study discusses healthy aging and typical aging. Because these volumes cover many years and are ongoing, they will be useful for graduate students, researchers, and professionals in the field of gerontology.

Rosow, Irving. *Socialization to Old Age*. Berkeley and Los Angeles, CA: University of California Press, 1974. 188p. OP. ISBN 0-520-02461-3.

In this concise book, the author uses concepts in role theory to explore entry into old age and what this entails in U.S. society. The author argues that old age is characterized by role losses and ambiguities in norms and generally paints a negative picture of this period of life. Rosow uses an extensive review of relevant literature to support his argument. This text was written for a sociological audience and provides a theoretical basis from which practical applications may be made.

Schneider, Edward L., and John W. Rowe, eds. *Handbook of the Biology of Aging.* 3rd ed. New York: Harcourt Brace, 1989. 489p. $79.50. ISBN 0-12-627870-9.

For researchers and students, this revised second edition updates important issues previously examined and covers new areas pertinent to human aging such as geriatric medicine, exercise, the neurochemistry of aging, physiology, and modulation of aging processes. It also critically evaluates interventions that have been suggested to alter aging.

Scott-Maxwell, Florida. *The Measure of My Days.* New York: Knopf, 1968. $9.95; $5.95. ISBN 0-394-43565-6; 0-14-005164-3, paper.

In another little classic reminiscence, Florida Scott-Maxwell records her eighty-third year. She is English, living alone in a flat (where she lived until her death at 95), and her eighty-third year is not a lucky one. Recounting her losses and sorrows, she writes about the year as one of discovery. Those approaching aging, and fearing it, would do well to read this little gem by an old woman coming to terms with herself.

U.S. Bureau of the Census, Center for International Research. *An Aging World.* International Population Reports, Series P-95, #78. Washington, DC: Government Printing Office, 1987. 85p. $5.50. Stock No. 003-024-06699-8.

By the year 2000, more than 410 million people in the world are expected to be 65 years of age or over compared with 290 million today. These and other demographic changes in the aged population worldwide are reported in *An Aging World,* a demographic study of population growth and change in 31 countries. Of significant concern to planners all over the world is that the oldest old—those aged 80 or over—are the fastest growing component of the elderly population. These data on the world's elderly, including life expectancy, mortality and health, marital status, educational attainment, social support, and the economics of aging, will have significance for planners and researchers needing hard-to-find international statistics.

U.S. Bureau of the Census. *Current Population Reports.* Washington, DC: Government Printing Office, various years.

These reports provide continuing, up-to-date statistics on population counts, characteristics, and other special studies. The following is a list of specific series that may be of interest.

> Series P-20, Population Characteristics. Variously priced. Stock No. 803-005-00000-1.
>
> Series P-23, Special Studies. Variously priced. Stock No. 803-005-00000-1.
>
> Series P-25, Population Estimates and Projections. 20/yr. Individual reports have varying prices. Stock No. 803-004-00000-5.
>
> Series P-60, Consumer Income. Variously priced. Stock No. 803-004-00000-1.

Series P-20, P-23, and P-60 cost $96/year for a package of the three series. Individual reports within the series vary in price.

PERIODICALS

Ageing International. 2/yr. $17, individuals. $25, institutions and libraries. $12, students and retirees. International Federation on Ageing, 1909 K Street, NW, Washington, DC 20049. Available in English and Spanish editions.

This biannual journal of the International Federation on Ageing provides news briefs and analytical reports on significant worldwide trends in aging. Stories on topics such as age discrimination policies in Great Britain and Norway, retirement practices in Japan, and development loans to older women in Bangladesh make this publication a good way to compare what is happening in aging in other lands with what is happening in the United States. It is published in English and Spanish.

Aging Network News. 12/yr. $55. P.O. Box 1223, McLean, VA 22101.

Aging Network News transmits news exclusively about the U.S. network on aging. The monthly reports and analyses cover all the primary concerns in aging—long-term care, social supports, housing and environment, minority elderly, nutrition, older women, elder abuse, respite care, and Social Security, to name a few. Directed mainly to professionals working in the field of aging, it should appeal to health care providers, public policymakers, social service practitioners, and government agency personnel.

Aging Research & Training News. Biweekly. $147. 951 Pershing Drive, Silver Spring, MD 20910-4464.

This newsletter covers research and training opportunities, programs, grants, and contracts in the field of aging. There are reports on biomedical and social/behavioral research and news briefs gathered from federal agencies with interests in aging—the National Institute on Aging (NIA), the Administration on Aging (AoA), the Health Care Financing Administration (HCFA), the Census Bureau, and Congress, for example. This is an important source for up-to-date information on grant opportunities, NIA awards, publications and resources, and current regulations and legislation pertaining to the elderly—information needed by academics, researchers, and specialists in the field.

The Gerontologist. Bimonthly. $45. Gerontological Society of America, 1275 K Street, NW, Suite 350, Washington, DC 20005.

This refereed journal published by the Gerontological Society of America (GSA) is for the professional practitioner. It emphasizes clinical research and program applications, with articles divided into such categories as health care, housing, economics, history of gerontology, and ethnicity and race. There are signed book and audiovisual reviews. An annual special issue provides the program and abstracts of papers from the annual meeting of the GSA. Targeted to academia and the specialist, this journal keeps abreast of developments in the field.

Gray Panther Network. 4/yr. $15, individuals. $30, institutions and libraries. 311 South Juniper Street, Philadelphia, PA 19107.

This tabloid-format newspaper reports on current issues and activities of the Gray Panthers and other activist groups. Though it is primarily concerned with the issues of age discrimination and empowerment, there are also reports about legislation (both federal and state) and about activities at political conventions, peace rallies, and the regional grass-roots chapters. The Gray Panthers is made up of people of all ages, not just the elderly, and their newspaper will interest the general public as well as older adults.

Highlights. 6/yr. Free. American Association of Retired Persons, Field Services Department, 1909 K Street, NW, Washington, DC 20049.

While the emphasis is on social services, programs, and publications available to older Americans, considerable attention is devoted to health care issues and legislation. Recent issues have examined cost containment initiatives, Medicare coverage, physician assignment lists, and home safety programs.

The International Journal of Aging and Human Development: A Journal of Psychosocial Gerontology. 8/yr. $54, individuals. $106, institutions. Baywood Publishing Co., P.O. Box 337, Amityville, NY 11701.

This journal explores the implications of gerontological research for our understanding of the total development of the human organism. It presents international research on psychological and social studies of aging and the aged, which will interest academics and specialists in the field. Articles have reported studies on such topics as the relationship between health and life satisfaction, aging and attractiveness, and discouraged older workers.

Journal of Gerontology. Bimonthly. $45, individuals. $75, institutions. Gerontological Society of America, 1275 K Street, NW, Suite 350, Washington, DC 20005.

This is a basic journal in the field of gerontology, one of two published by the Gerontological Society of America (GSA). It is research oriented and includes articles on the problems of aging from the biological, medical, psychological, and social science perspectives. Most articles report original research. There are signed book reviews and an annual bibliography titled "Doctoral Dissertations on Aging from American Institutions of Higher Learning," which supplements the original work of the same name covering the years 1934–1969. This journal along with *The Gerontologist* provides a wide range of material in the field of gerontology.

Mature Outlook. Bimonthly. $6, members. $9, nonmembers. Mature Outlook, West Lake Avenue, Glenview, IL 60025.

This is a general-interest magazine from a national member organization for people over 50 that is sponsored by Sears Roebuck. Published for information and entertainment, it includes articles on travel, sports, food, people, health, and investment topics. This is an inexpensive general magazine for older adults.

Modern Maturity. 6/yr. $5. Free with membership in AARP. American Association of Retired Persons (AARP), 3200 East Carson Street, Lakewood, CA 90712.

This is certainly the best-known general magazine for those over 50. With an emphasis on the quality of living for older people today, its contents are the same as in any general magazine—travel, finance, health, fitness, and interviews (with older adults). Consumer information, reports from local AARP chapters, and updates on federal legislation of interest to seniors round out each issue. *Modern Maturity* has the largest circulation of any general-interest magazine of this genre. It's a good idea to have it in a core collection for those individuals who are not already receiving it and have heard it referred to often.

National Center for Health Statistics. *Advance Data from Vital and Health Statistics.* Irregular. Free. National Center for Health Statistics, 3700 East-West Highway, Hyattsville, MD 20782.

As the title suggests, this is the early release of selected data from health surveys that are later published in *Vital and Health Statistics Series.*

———. *Monthly Vital Statistics Report.* Monthly. Free. National Center for Health Statistics, 3700 East-West Highway, Hyattsville, MD 20782.

These monthly reports contain provisional data on vital statistics. Final data are presented in supplementary issues on particular topics.

———. *Vital and Health Statistics Series.* (Popularly known as the *Rainbow Series.*) Irregular. $1.00–$2.50. National Center for Health Statistics, 3700 East-West Highway, Hyattsville, MD 20782.

The most used in this group are series 10 and 11, which cover the National Interview Survey and the National Health and Nutrition Examination Survey (HANES), respectively. These two series contain nationwide prevalence data on chronic diseases. Series 13 contains data on facilities providing long-term care, ambulatory care, and hospital care. Recent reports in series 3, *Analytical Studies,* cover changes in mortality among the elderly and health statistics for older persons.

New Choices for the Best Years. 12/yr. $15. New Choices, P.O. Box 1945, Marion, OH 43302.

New Choices is a special-interest magazine for the over-50 age group. Formerly titled *Fifty Plus,* it is now a Reader's Digest publication that stresses how to get the most out of the middle years. It is written in a popular style for the general reader with articles on travel, housing, hobbies, nutrition, health, money, and people who exemplify over 50 as the best years of life.

Alcohol and Drug Abuse

BOOKS

Atkinson, Roland M., ed. *Alcohol and Drug Abuse in Old Age.* Washington, DC: American Psychiatric Press, 1984. 70p. $12. ISBN 0-88048-050-5.

Alcohol and drug problems tend to be associated with youth and younger adults. This book shows that the elderly also experience significant problems with substance abuse and summarizes the information in a manner useful to students, teachers, and practitioners. The authors emphasize clinical themes rather than sociological or neuro-scientific aspects. Papers address the many special features of alcohol and drug abuse in old age, diagnosis and treatment of alcoholism, and the use of over-the-counter drugs and interaction of multiple drugs. The book concludes with the hope that there will be more identification of the problems of substance abuse in the elderly, because treatment outcome can be surprisingly good.

Gottheil, Edward, et al., eds. *The Combined Problems of Alcoholism, Drug Addiction and Aging.* Springfield, IL: Charles Thomas, 1985. 360p. $48.25. ISBN 0-398-05046-5.

This collection of papers presented at the 1983 Coatesville-Jefferson conference by researchers and practitioners probes the basic issues of substance addiction, analyzes its occurrence in the aged, and maps out approaches to the older addict. The papers specifically address psychosocial aspects of aging and substance abuse, drug use and misuse by the elderly, coping tactics of elderly substance abusers, and treatment strategies. These reports will be of interest to all who work or live with elderly addicts and will provide help in reaching and treating them.

Lipton, Helen L., and Philip R. Lee. *Drugs and the Elderly: Clinical, Social and Policy Perspectives*. Stanford, CA: Stanford University Press, 1988. 263p. $35. IBSN 0-8047-1295-6.

This book analyzes the current state of knowledge of the field of geriatric drug use, ranging from how drugs act in the aging body, to the role of the Food and Drug Administration in the testing and marketing of drugs, to how and why the elderly use (and misuse) their drugs. It also points out areas where more research is needed. Particularly notable are the strategies the authors propose for alleviating the problems that have been identified. This action agenda makes this a valuable book for health policymakers; for instructors, particularly in pharmacy, medicine, dentistry, and nursing; for practitioners; for social and behavioral scientists interested in geriatrics; and for consumers interested in the issues related to drugs and the elderly.

Maddox, George, et al., eds. *Nature and Extent of Alcohol Problems among the Elderly*. New York: Springer, 1986. 331p. $36.95. ISBN 0-8261-5480-8.

This volume is one of a series of research monographs from the National Institute on Alcohol Abuse and Alcoholism. The papers include such topics as recovery in older alcoholics, alcohol and nutrition, and the interaction of medication and alcohol. There are reports on data from longitudinal studies and on data on alcohol consumption and alcohol problems among different age groups. This volume is a valuable contribution to information about drinking behavior among the elderly and as such will be useful for health service providers, administrators, and researchers interested in alcohol problems in the elderly.

Mishara, Brian L., and Robert Kastenbaum. *Alcohol and Old Age*. New York: Grune & Stratton, 1980. 220p. $39.50. ISBN 0-8089-1226-7.

The authors, both professionals in mental health, note here the variety of opinions about alcohol and old age. Some feel alcohol is dangerous at any age, in any amount, and that it is even more dangerous in old age. The opposing position suggests that alcohol has therapeutic potential for older people and its consumption should be encouraged. This book attempts to develop perspective on both the use and abuse theories and identify areas where research and clinical effort could usefully be directed. Physicians, nurses, social workers, ministers, nursing home administrators, and others concerned with the well-being of the elderly will find useful information in the chapters on problem drinking in old age, methods of treating alcohol problems, the physiological effects of alcoholic beverages, and a historical survey of the past several millennia of alcohol use by older persons.

Moore, Steven R., and Thomas W. Teel, eds. *Geriatric Drug Use—Chemical and Social Perspectives*. New York: Pergamon Press, 1985. 222p. $32. ISBN 0-08-031939-4.

These edited proceedings of a 1984 workshop on geriatric drug use offer an excellent balance of concerns in the areas of social policy, patient care, biomedical research, and government-industry relations. The contributors discuss such issues as drug labeling, physician instructions to the patient, self-medication with over-the-counter drugs, clinical tests, risk factors in geriatric drug use, research, and health promotion. Health professionals, organizations, agencies, and older consumers and their caregivers will find information here to help them solve problems of drug misuse and abuse among the elderly.

Alzheimer's Disease, Dementias, and Brain Disease

BOOKS AND GOVERNMENT PUBLICATIONS

Fraser, Virginia, and Susan M. Thornton. *Understanding "Senility": A Layperson's Guide*. Buffalo, NY: Prometheus Books, 1987. 103p. OP. ISBN 0-87975-391-9; 0-87975-392-7, paper.

This booklet had its beginnings when the mother of one of the authors had what we now know to be Alzheimer's disease. Once, when trying to understand her mother's behavior, the author was told, "What do you expect? Your mother is 84!" This book was written to help others desperate for a description of what they were facing. The authors provide very basic information to families, friends, and caregivers; explore early symptoms and later behavior patterns of those with Alzheimer's disease; and describe treatable conditions that are sometimes mistaken for Alzheimer's. A bibliography and resource list is also provided for further reading and to help in locating relevant support services.

Henig, Robin M. *The Myth of Senility: The Truth about the Brain and Aging*. Washington, DC: American Association of Retired Persons and Scott, Foresman, 1988. 198p. $14.95. ISBN 0-673-24892-5.

Perhaps the greatest myth about senility is the belief that confusion, disorientation, memory loss, and lack of concentration are a natural and unavoidable result of aging. They aren't. These symptoms actually indicate a condition called dementia, which is quite often treatable and reversible. The author has assembled a body of medical data to help readers understand that many dementia symptoms are a result of such causes as improper nutrition or side effects of medications, that most older persons retain their intelligence throughout life, and that "the old mind is like an old muscle" that must be used and challenged in order to function well. Anyone who is old, knows old people, or is becoming old and is worried about "senility" will be reassured by this book.

Jarvik, Lissy F., and Carol H. Winograd, eds. *Treatments for the Alzheimer Patient: The Long Haul.* New York: Springer, 1988. 272p. $28.95. ISBN 0-8261-6000-X.

The contributors to this volume focus on Alzheimer's disease and related disorders as diseases that can be helped rather than as hopeless conditions. The chapters encompass diagnosis, treatment and behavioral management, family assessment and support, and community involvement. Each encourages treatment of Alzheimer's patients and provides up-to-date information about treatment options. Although the book is geared to health professionals in a variety of disciplines, laypersons working with, caring for, or interested in Alzheimer's patients will find it accessible.

Jorm, A. *A Guide to the Understanding of Alzheimer's Disease and Related Disorders.* New York: New York University Press, 1987. 158p. $32.00; $12.50. ISBN 0-8147-4170-3; 0-8147-4174-6, paper.

This collection of 12 review articles—on topics ranging from etiology to impact on families and public policy to assessment and management—communicates the expanding knowledge of dementia in a clear, concise manner to the nonspecialist. Whatever the topic, Jorm makes the central point; identifies the major issues; and provides the key references, tables, figures, and/or assessment instruments. A 12-page reference list allows readers to pursue particular topics in depth. This book could be of value to health care practitioners and to caregiving families who want more information about dementia.

Sheridan, Carmel. *Failure-Free Activities for the Alzheimer's Patient: A Guidebook for Caregivers.* Oakland, CA: Cottage Books, 1987. 104p. $9.95. ISBN 0-943873-05-3.

The aim of this book is to offer simple activities that help reinforce the patient's self-esteem while relieving boredom and frustration. The activities described may be used by all who come in contact with the Alzheimer's patient: the family caregiver, the companion, the nurse's aide, or the occasional visitor. Possibilities include music, exercise, baking cookies, gardening, and activities involving children. The emphasis is on assets rather than deficits, and caregivers will be pleased to find such practical activities to enhance the life of Alzheimer's sufferers.

U.S. Congress, Office of Technology Assessment. *Confused Minds, Burdened Families: Finding Help for People with Alzheimer's Disease and Other Dementias.* Washington, DC: Government Printing Office, 1990. In press.

This report, commissioned by six congressional committees, is a follow-up to the previous report by the Office of Technology Assessment, *Losing a Million Minds.* It centers on problems in locating and arranging for services, showing that the needs of dementia victims and their families are so diverse that the system must be able to refer them to a wide range of services. It calls for development of a comprehensive national service system that goes beyond information and referral to provide outreach and case management to dementia victims and their caregivers.

———. *Losing a Million Minds: Confronting the Tragedy of Alzheimer's Disease and Other Dementias.* Washington, DC: Government Printing Office, 1987. 539p. $15. Stock No. 052-003-01072-1.

In response to congressional concern about Alzheimer's disease and other dementias, the Office of Technology Assessment prepared this excellent report. This document reflects the diversity of issues associated with dementia—the disease, the family, long-term care services, patient assessment, financing long-term care for persons with dementia, and biomedical research policy. Although written at the request of Congress to provide information for policymakers, this document contains a wealth of material for anyone interested in dementias, including professionals and laypeople.

Zarit, Steven H., Nancy K. Orr, and Judy M. Zarit. *The Hidden Victims of Alzheimer's Disease: Families under Stress.* New York: New York University

Alzeimer's Disease, Dementias, Brain Disease

Press, 1985. 218p. $32.50; $15.00. ISBN 0-8147-9662-1; 0-8147-9663-X, paper.

Using case examples, these authors tell professionals how to help families care for an Alzheimer's patient. They show how to respond to situations such as stealing, incontinence, asking repetitive questions, and inappropriate public behavior. They offer a step-by-step guide to caring for an Alzheimer's victim at home and management of dementia-related behavior. This is a valuable book for those helping families who are struggling with the stresses of Alzheimer's.

Zgola, Jitka M. *Doing Things: A Guide to Programming Activities for Persons with Alzheimer's Disease and Related Disorders.* Baltimore, MD: Johns Hopkins University Press, 1987. 149p. $20.00; $8.95. ISBN 0-8018-3467-8; 0-8018-3466-X, paper.

Doing Things is written primarily for professionals working in group programs. It begins with an overview of Alzheimer's patients' abilities and deficits to help professionals design a program based on patients' strengths and needs. The book discusses and illustrates a variety of activities, specifying objectives, scheduling, pacing, and staff requirements. Zgola suggests techniques for presenting activities, coping with failure, and handling problem behaviors. Based on the experience of a successful daycare program, this book provides information, ideas, and step-by-step instructions for satisfying activities for cognitively impaired adults.

PERIODICAL

American Journal of Alzheimer's Care and Related Disorders & Research. 6/yr. $52. 470 Boston Post Road, Weston, MA 02193.

This professional journal publishes articles about Alzheimer's care and research focusing on topics such as environmental design for dementia, the risk of Alzheimer's for relatives of patients, medications, behavior management, and legal issues. It also includes book reviews, news briefs, and conference announcements. Since this is currently the sole journal for professionals in Alzheimer's care and research, it is a useful addition to any core collection.

VIDEOCASSETTES

Caregiving with Grace
Type: ½" VHS and Beta videocassette, color
Length: 28 min.

Date: 1987
Cost: Purchase $400, rental $100
Source: Video Services
Department of Physical Therapy
University of Maryland
School of Medicine
32 South Greene Street
Baltimore, MD 21201

Caregiving with Grace, the sequel to *Living with Grace,* is about an Alzheimer's victim in the later stages of her disease. Grace now needs constant supervision and considerable assistance with activities of daily living. She rarely speaks and does not follow conversations. Videotaped ten years after the initial diagnosis, this documentary shares both practical and emotional solutions reached by her husband and a foster home as they provide daily care for Grace. Used in conjunction with *Living with Grace,* this program provides the opportunity to observe the progression of Alzheimer's disease and the resulting modifications necessary in caregiving.

Living with Grace
Type: ½" VHS and Beta videocassette, color
Length: 28 min.
Date: 1984
Cost: Purchase $400, rental $100
Source: Video Services
Department of Physical Therapy
University of Maryland
School of Medicine
32 South Greene Street
Baltimore, MD 21201

Living with Grace explores the life of one woman suffering from Alzheimer's disease—her loss of memory, emotional mood swings, catastrophic reactions, and confusion. Filmed over a period of five months, this documentary presents her life at home with her caring husband, his efforts, and the solutions arrived at so that their lives can continue with dignity and meaning. Made six years after the initial diagnosis, this superb, prize-winning video should be viewed by everyone who works with or cares for someone with Alzheimer's disease or a related disorder.

Caregiving

BOOKS AND GOVERNMENT PUBLICATIONS

Chapman, Elwood N. *The Unfinished Business of Living: Helping Aging Parents Help Themselves.* Los Altos, CA: Crisp Publications, 1988. 232p. $12.95. ISBN 0-931961-19-X.

Family communication and relationships are the focal point of *The Unfinished Business of Living.* The format is that of a workbook, with family studies at the end of each chapter that are excellent for group discussion or self-instruction. Specific family communication exercises and sample forms useful for the business aspects of caregiving make this a highly practical book for all family members dealing with decisions involving the well-being of the elderly.

Edinberg, Mark A. *Talking with Your Aging Parents.* Boston, MA: Shambhala Publications, 1987. 220p. $9.95. ISBN 0-87773-440-2.

Edinberg offers the adult child practical skills, strategies, and support for discussing important issues such as failing health, financial and legal matters, and family relations with aging parents. He explores how communication styles can help or hinder family discussions and shows how adult children can clarify their purposes when talking with their parents, appreciate their parents' responses, and understand the implications of choices such as concealing information or making decisions for their parents. There are warning signs throughout the book to let readers know when talking with parents may not go well and something else needs to be done. This book is not a guide about finding and utilizing services for older persons, but it is an excellent guide for all family members attempting to handle important yet frequently difficult discussions with older relatives.

Hooyman, Nancy R., and Wendy Lustbader. *Taking Care: Supporting Older People and Their Families.* New York: Free Press, 1986. 322p. $24.95. ISBN 0-02-914900-2.

Recognizing the fact that families provide 80 percent of in-home care for the elderly and that the number of families providing this care will increase as the aged population increases, the authors provide solutions to the problems caregivers face. They explain the physical and mental changes associated with aging and the emotional strains on family members. They examine such issues as abusive caregiving relationships, lesbian and gay relationships, an older person's wish to die, and overcoming an older person's resistance toward using services. Family caregivers, health professionals, social workers, and members of the clergy will find this book useful. It also includes checklists and specific interview questions for families hiring live-in help.

Horne, Jo. *Caregiving: Helping an Aging Loved One.* Washington, DC: American Association of Retired Persons and Scott, Foresman, 1985. 334p. $13.95. ISBN 0-673-24822-4.

Based on the author's research and experience as administrator of an adult daycare facility, this book helps those who are caring for an aging loved one to identify the type of assistance that could help them deal with problems and stress. It provides advice about handling financial and legal matters, coping with the elder's disorientation, and solving exercise and hygiene problems of the care recipient. It also includes case histories to aid in recognizing and coping with emotional burdens common to both the aging person and the caregiver—such feelings as guilt, anger, frustration, exhaustion, anxiety, fear, and sadness. This volume is both a specific reference tool and a general handbook for caregivers.

How To Hire Helpers: A Guide for Elders and Their Families. Seattle, WA: Church Council of Greater Seattle, 1988. 11p. $3. No ISBN.

The Task Force on Aging of the Church Council of Greater Seattle prepared this guide in response to community concerns about older persons being victims of fraudulent, abusive, or poorly qualified workers. It is aimed at older persons and their families who contemplate hiring someone to assist periodically with household routine and personal care. It is not intended for those looking for live-in care. This extremely helpful step-by-step guide includes sample advertisements, interview questions, and tips for keeping workers once you've found them. A discount is given for multiple copies.

Jarvik, Lissy, and Gary Small. *Parentcare: A Commonsense Guide for Adult Children.* New York: Crown Publishers, 1988. 309p. $19.95. ISBN 0-517-56765-2.

Written for a general audience and for adult children, as the title indicates, the authors' "commonsense approach to problem solving" offers a clear way to think about problems that arise when taking care of elderly parents. Topics include relationships, money, food, work, sex, health, and housing.

Parentcare has a clear writing style, charts that highlight the main points of each chapter, and case examples. There are almost 100 pages of appendices about common health problems, side effects of anti-depressants, information about living wills and powers of attorney, and suggested reading. This is a detailed and factual resource book for both the adult child and parents planning their own future.

Mace, Nancy L., and Peter V. Rabins. *The 36-Hour Day: A Family Guide to Caring for Persons with Alzheimer's Disease, Related Dementing Illness, and Memory Loss in Later Life*. New York: Warner Books, 1989. 253p. $5.95. ISBN 0-446-35786-3, paper.

The 36-Hour Day was written specifically for the families of persons victimized by incurable dementing illnesses—those for whom caring for an afflicted family member can make every day seem 36 hours long. The authors prepare the family for all aspects of home care—including problems such as disorientation, personality changes, and loss of coordination—and suggest ways the family can help protect the impaired relative from household hazards and self-injury. Although there are numerous newer books on the subject of caring for dementia victims, this book is still the best at examining the feelings and tensions that affect the family itself. The authors' understanding view of the anger, shame, guilt, and frustration that everyone experiences at some time in this situation makes this an invaluable guide for the home care of those in the early and middle stages of dementing illness.

Miles Away and Still Caring: A Guide for Long-Distance Caregivers. Washington, DC: American Association of Retired Persons, 1986. 17p. Single issue free. No ISBN.

Many Americans today face the task of coordinating care for an aged relative who lives in another town or state. This booklet helps long-distance caregivers identify problem areas, discover resources for support, and create a network of assistance. The recommendations cover topics such as housing, nutrition, legal problems, health care costs, and mental health evaluation. There is also advice for dealing with the social services network. Anyone working with caregivers of the elderly should have a stock of this useful guide to give away.

Norris, Jane, ed. *Daughters of the Elderly: Building Partnerships in Caregiving*. Bloomington, IN: Indiana University Press, 1988. 223p. $27.50; $9.95, paper. ISBN 0-253-31612-X; 0-253-20484-4, paper.

In *Daughters of the Elderly,* eight daughters (and one son) share the stories of their struggles and successes with the difficult task of caring for an elderly parent. There are stories of daily care, personal growth and physical decay, deepening family ties, the ache of letting go, and the importance of finding support in the community and of sharing burdens. After each personal narrative, a professional addresses selected issues including support and advocacy for the elderly, decision making in health care, well-being, and self-care. Written for family caregivers, the book includes lists of suggested readings and a glossary of some of the specialized terminology used in aging-related circles.

Shelley, Florence D. *When Your Parents Grow Old.* New York: Harper & Row, 1988. 416p. $22.95. ISBN 0-06-055010-4.

Written for those who are caring for a parent, this book contains valuable advice on improving the quality of the aging parent's life. The author covers home care versus nursing home care, money matters, doctors, hospitals and health maintenance organizations (HMOs), diseases and disorders of the elderly, and community agencies and organizations that can help the caregiver. This is a practical, informative resource that can help readers anticipate and deal with the frailties that aging often brings.

Silverstone, Barbara, and Helen K. Hyman. *You and Your Aging Parent: The Modern Family's Guide to Emotional, Physical, and Financial Problems.* 3rd ed. New York: Pantheon Books, 1989. 361p. $24.95; $12.95, paper. ISBN 0-394-57741-8; 0-679-72154-0, paper.

You and Your Aging Parent was one of the earliest books written for the general public on being a family caregiver. The first section, "Taking Stock," presents an overall review of the range of problems that may complicate life for the elderly and their children—typical losses of old age. The second section, "Taking Action," analyzes available solutions to the problems raised in the earlier chapters: how to find community programs, how to evaluate nursing facilities, and how to pay for care. The appendix contains a bibliography, including directories of essential services, and an overall guide to specialized agencies and services, both public and private, across the nation. Despite the current plethora of titles on family caregiving, the newly revised *You and Your Aging Parent* is still among the most useful.

Sommers, Tish, and Laurie Shields. *Women Take Care: The Consequences of Caregiving in Today's Society.* Gainesville, FL: Triad Publishing Co.,

1987. 224p. $16.95; $9.95, paper. ISBN 0-937404-28-4; 0-937404-27-6, paper.

Founders of the Older Women's League (OWL), the authors focus on the fact that the burden of family caregiving usually falls on women. They set forth the realities of growing old and of caregiving, provide suggestions for dealing with some of the practical problems, and propose a nationally supported program to reduce the economic burden on family caregivers. They describe the emotional, financial, physical, social, and legal burdens women face as caregivers and include a resource appendix with addresses and written guides to help women in a practical way. Their call for political action by women's groups reflects their conviction that changing the situation of caregivers involves confronting national priorities.

Stephens, Susan A., and Jon B. Christianson. *Informal Care of the Elderly.* New York: Lexington Books, 1986. 174p. $20. ISBN 0-669-11227-5.

Between February 1982 and October 1984, a federally funded project known as the national Long-Term Care Demonstration provided additional services in ten states to persons believed to be at risk of being institutionalized. This book reports findings regarding the informal care network established. Caregivers were found to be spending 40 hours per week with the recipient and another 28 hours in caregiving activities. The majority of care was given by spouses, followed by daughters and daughters-in-law. This well-written and documented report is for academic libraries and professionals working with caregivers.

Stone, Robyn. *Exploding the Myths. Caregiving in America: A Study.* Washington, DC: U.S. Congress, House Select Committee on Aging, 1987. 73p. $2.50. Stock No. 052-070-06342-4.

This document is often quoted and cited in the literature on the subject of caregiving. It is an overview of issues related to families providing care for the elderly. The chapters provide background on demographic and social trends that are placing increased demands on eldercare, characteristics and problems of family caregivers, and federal legislation related to informal caregiving. It emphasizes the continued contributions of the family in providing care and the increasing problems in coping with caregiving responsibilities.

Tomb, David A. *Growing Old: A Handbook for You and Your Aging Parent.* New York: Viking, 1984. 397p. $19.95. ISBN 0-670-11038-8.

This informative guide focuses on the major topics of interest to caregivers—the physical changes and psychological and medical problems associated with growing old. It shows how to promote good health and prevent illness, describes family relationships, and outlines the realities of housing, finances, recreation, education, the law, and dying. Of all the guides for caregivers that have been published, Tomb's is one of the very few that is medically oriented in its focus on the aged person and the aging process. It will be especially useful to new caregivers.

PERIODICALS

Parent Care: Resources To Assist Family Caregivers. 6/yr. $20. Parent Care, Gerontology Center, 316 Strong Hall, The University of Kansas, Lawrence, KS 66045.

Parent Care finds and analyzes program developments, research findings, and other resources for caregivers of the elderly. Information on community services, living arrangements, health issues, support networks, nursing homes, and death and dying fills each issue along with useful suggestions for books, videos, and special reports that can bring the reader added information. This newsletter will greatly assist caregivers in discovering new resources, keeping up-to-date on the latest research, and learning from others in similar situations.

AUDIOVISUAL RESOURCES

The Dollmaker
Type: Slides/audiotape
Length: 17 min.
Date: 1987
Cost: $47.50 plus $3.50 postage/handling
Source: Vicky Schmall
          Oregon State University Extension Service
          161 Milam Hall
          Corvallis, OR 97331-5106

A woman who has made dolls for many years is portrayed devoting her life to her husband as he becomes senile. Shortly thereafter she dies and he goes to live with his daughter's family. As his condition worsens, the family seeks professional help. Advised that they cannot let the function of taking care of the father disrupt their own marriage and family, they explore alternative care facilities. The philosophical implications of providing a professional facility are discussed as the family comes to view the problems of an aging parent in a positive way.

My Mother, My Father
Type: 16mm film, ½" VHS videocassette, color
Length: 33 min.
Date: 1984
Cost: Film rental $495; VHS purchase $395, rental $50
Source: Terra Nova Films, Inc.
          9848 South Winchester Avenue
          Chicago, IL 60643

This prize-winning film shows four real-life families, each struggling in their own way with the stresses and changes involved in caring for a frail older parent. The Honel family cares for their father, who has Alzheimer's, at home. The Hagwoods make use of adult daycare, the Gerali family supports their mother's decision to live with a widowed daughter, and the Tjerdemas struggle with family conflict in a decision about their mother. This very candid documentary does not provide answers but will facilitate discussion for caregivers, health care professionals, clergy, community groups, students of gerontology and geriatrics, and counselors.

Death, Dying, and Hospice

BOOKS

Campbell, Scott, and Phyllis R. Silverman. *Widower.* New York: Prentice-Hall, 1987. 227p. $17.95. ISBN 0-13-959503-1.

Statistics show that widowed men are more vulnerable than other men to serious psychological disorders, health problems, and possibly an earlier death. Through firsthand accounts, this work illustrates the various ways in which men have successfully come to grips with the loss of a spouse. The author analyzes these experiences and offers ways to work through the grieving process. There is advice for starting self-help or widower groups along with directories of such groups and of other helpful organizations. Because so little has been written from the perspective of the widower, this is an important addition to any collection on aging.

Chase, Deborah. *Dying at Home with Hospice.* St. Louis, MO: C. V. Mosby, 1986. 204p. OP. ISBN 0-8016-0959-3.

Hospice, of course, is a philosophy, not a building. The author presents the entire framework for caring both for the dying and the family of the dying by describing the different types of hospice programs, the financial aspects of hospice care, daily care needs, and the legal and financial aspects of death at home. The final chapter lists hospice programs available nationwide. This practical guide offers help to the layperson and his or her family.

Clifford, Dennis. *Plan Your Estate.* Berkeley, CA: Nolo Press, 1989. 220p. $17.95. ISBN 0-87337-050-3.

This is a how-to book, although the author is careful to flag situations that require professional help. He discusses tax considerations, gifts, and probate avoidance devices such as living trusts. Wills, durable powers of attorney, living wills, and organ donations are explained, and the author includes sample estate plans. The book is well written, provides concrete examples, and will serve the general reader as a balanced estate planning guide.

Coleman, Barbara. *A Consumer Guide to Hospice Care.* Washington, DC: National Consumers League, 1990. 25p. $6. No ISBN.

This guide is designed to provide information to the public on both the benefits and disadvantages of hospice care, to help individuals and their families make informed decisions. It describes hospice services and organizations, explains how the costs of hospice care are covered, and describes the standards that exist for hospices. The guide also includes descriptions of two hospice organizations and case studies of two families who went through a hospice program.

Loewinsohn, Ruth Jean. *Survival Handbook for Widows (and for Relatives and Friends Who Want To Understand).* Washington, DC: American Association of Retired Persons, 1984. 141p. $5.95. ISBN 0-673-2420-8.

In the *Survival Handbook for Widows,* Loewinsohn describes common experiences from the moment a widow learns of her husband's death to the time—months or even years later—when she can feel like a whole person again. Detailed advice is given on settling claims and on estate planning. There are exercises for letting go of the past and ideas for getting started on living in the present and planning for the future. Although this book is about and for widows, widowers face the same problems and will find the book helpful as well.

Myers, Edward. *When Parents Die: A Guide for Adults.* New York: Viking, 1986. 208p. $13.95. ISBN 0-670-80771-0.

When Parents Die addresses the psychological and practical realities of the death of a parent and offers the comfort and information needed to make the experience less stressful, complex, and exhausting. The book examines the basic psychology of mourning and parental loss and provides concrete suggestions for dealing with these issues. The author discusses the medical and financial effects of a parent's death as well as the emotional fallout and lists resources for counseling and further reading and information. Although written primarily for readers whose parents have already died, the book will also be useful during a parent's illness.

Nelson, Thomas C. *It's Your Choice: The Practical Guide to Planning a Funeral.* Washington, DC: American Association of Retired Persons, 1987. 128p. $4.95. ISBN 0-673-24804-6.

This book is a clearheaded guide to making funeral arrangements and can be used for reference as well as a guide for making one's wishes known. There are choices about many of the services included (and charged for) in a funeral home's traditional package; people can have a funeral without the cost of a funeral director. Most people make funeral arrangements under the pressure of grief or shock, so the author encourages thinking ahead and discusses many of the details one must know when planning a funeral. This is a very useful book to help plan for a difficult time.

Silverman, Phyllis. *Widow-to-Widow.* Vol. 7 of the Springer Series on Social Work. New York: Springer, 1986. 227p. $24.95. ISBN 0-8261-5030-6.

This is a book about women as widows and about widows helping other widows. The various chapters bring together current research on bereavement, the psychology of women, the problems of the widow, and the effects of mutual-help interventions. Silverman presents the findings of the landmark Widow to Widow project carried out at Harvard from 1967 to 1973, which has been the basis for the growing number of mutual-help programs for widows. Those interested in mutual/self-help approaches to widowhood will find this book readable and practical.

Soled, Alex J. *The Essential Guide to Wills, Estates, Trusts and Death Taxes.* Washington, DC: American Association of Retired Persons and Scott, Foresman, 1986. 290p. $19.95; $12.95, paper. ISBN 0-673-24890-9; 0-673-24891-7, paper.

Soled, one of the nation's foremost experts on inheritance taxes, has written a book to help with estate planning. He answers such questions as: What is a living will? What should a will contain? When should probate be avoided? What about lawyer's fees? *The Essential Guide* is organized to permit quick reference to specific topics. Nearly 100 pages of appendices detail such information as the federal unified estate-tax rate, death taxes imposed by the various states, and how each state disposes of property in the absence of a will.

Stoddard, Sandol. *The Hospice Movement: A Better Way of Caring for the Dying.* Briarcliff Manor, NY: Stein and Day, 1978. 266p. $9.95. ISBN 0-8128-2178-5.

The author traces the history of the hospice movement from medieval times to the present day. She describes hospice programs in Great Britain and the United States, using personal stories and staff interviews to illustrate attitudes and concepts. Appendices list the drugs used to control pain in the two countries, and there is an extensive bibliography. Improved communication with the terminally ill and enlightened care of their needs has become a topic of great public interest, and this book will increase understanding of a subject that was, until recently, taboo.

Weizman, Savine G., and Phyllis Kamm. *About Mourning: Support and Guidance for the Bereaved.* New York: Human Sciences Press, 1985. 240p. $29.95; $16.95, paper. ISBN 0-89885-136-X; 0-89885-307-5, paper.

About Mourning will prove to be helpful and practical to many who are coping with the death of a loved one. While it is true that time tempers feelings of pain and sadness, these feelings do not go away. Mourners will not be cured of grief but they will be changed by it. The authors guide readers through this process, helping them understand their feelings and reactions. This book will help the bereaved and professionals who work with them.

Zimmerman, Jack M. *Hospice: Complete Care for the Terminally Ill.* 2nd ed. Baltimore, MD: Urban & Schwarzenberg, 1986. 311p. $34.50. ISBN 0-8067-2212-6.

Like the first edition, this book is designed to assist those who are developing a hospice program. The new edition includes information on Medicare hospice benefits and state regulations relating to hospice care. There are new chapters on the extension of the hospice concept to provide care for patients with nonmalignant terminal illnesses, such as AIDS and irreversible neurological conditions. Although this book is aimed at those involved in the early stages of a hospice program, anyone concerned with care of the terminally ill will find something of value.

PERIODICAL

The Hospice Journal: Psychological and Pastoral Care of the Dying. 4/yr. $30, individuals. $42, institutions. $75, libraries. Haworth Press, 10 Alice Street, Binghamton, NY 13904.

This journal is the official quarterly of the National Hospice Organization. It offers coverage of all aspects of care for the dying and their families with major emphasis on hospice care, but terminal care and bereavement care are also addressed. Some typical articles have been on the volunteer in bereavement work, nurses as primary spiritual care workers, and the role of imagery in treatment of a cancer patient. This journal is recommended for academics and specialists in the hospice movement.

VIDEOCASSETTE

The Right To Die . . . The Choice Is Yours
Type: ½" VHS videocassette, color
Length: 14 min.
Date: 1987
Cost: $29.95
Source: New York Society for the Right to Die
          250 West 57th Street
          New York, NY 10107

This videotape presents two cases: a younger person with juvenile diabetes who had dialysis withdrawn and subsequently died, and an older couple with multiple medical problems who have both signed living wills. Throughout these presentations the narrator makes various points concerning a person's rights and responsibilities when deciding on life-prolonging measures. The videotape is accompanied by a pamphlet with questions for discussion as well as a question-and-answer section concerning patients' rights, with specific emphasis on living wills. The videotape and pamphlet would be most useful as an education tool for patients and their families.

Economics and Insurance

BOOKS AND GOVERNMENT PUBLICATIONS

Altman, Maya, et al. *How Do I Pay for My Long-Term Health Care? A Consumer Guidebook about Long-Term Care Insurance.* Berkeley, CA: Berkeley Planning Associates, 1988. 106p. $12.95. ISBN 0-9620825-0-3.

Written for consumers and professionals concerned with personal financial planning and long-term health care, this guidebook is an ideal reference for retirees, pre-retirees and their families, benefit counselors, case managers, nurses and physicians, estate planners, and other financial advisors. Plainly written and up-to-date, this book explains what is meant by long-term care and whether Medicare and Medicare supplement insurance will pay for it, describes what options other than insurance will cover long-term care, and shows how to compare insurance policies.

Bernstein, Merton C., and Joan B. Bernstein. *Social Security: The System That Works.* New York: Basic Books, 1988. 321p. $21.95. ISBN 0-465-07916-4.

As can be gathered from the title, this book explains why Social Security will endure and why it could never be replaced in scope or reliability by any other pension plan. The authors—one is a law professor and a former consultant to the National Commission on Social Security Reform and the other is a nonprofit agency administrator—mount a knowledgeable defense of Social Security. They challenge the view that Social Security is inequitable and financially insecure and force policymakers and older citizens to think hard about designing the right mix of pensions for their future. There is a helpful glossary to Social Security terms such as COLA and OASI. This basic book is written for the layperson who is trying to understand the role of Social Security in his or her retirement.

Eastaugh, Steven R. *Financing Health Care: Economic Efficiency and Equity.* Dover, MA: Auburn House, 1987. 720p. $34.95; $17.95, paper. ISBN 0-86569-150-9; 0-86569-161-4, paper.

Written for managers, policymakers, health care providers, and graduate students, this book delves into medical economics and financial management from the point of view of corporations, hospitals, health maintenance organizations (HMOs), long-term care, and marketing. This leads to such topics as cost containment, marketing, pricing and specialization, quality assurance, efficiency, diversification, and future trends. This book will find an audience with those interested in currently available research results and potential policy ramifications.

Hogue, Kathleen, Cheryl Jensen, and Kathleen M. Urban. *The Complete Guide to Health Insurance: How To Beat the High Cost of Being Sick.* New York: Walker and Company, 1988. 363p. $24.95. ISBN 0-8027-1024-7.

This guide covers every major health insurance issue for the under-65 population as well as for older Americans. The authors answer the most commonly asked questions—what to do if you have no insurance, how to protect yourself against the cost of a catastrophic illness, and how much insurance is too much or not enough. All types of insurance—Medicare, Medicaid, and Blue Cross and other private commercial plans—are thoroughly examined. Well written and easy to understand, the guide will give consumers practical strategies needed to make informed health insurance decisions.

Income of the Population 55 and Over. Biennial. $5.50. Social Security Administration, Office of Research Statistics, Room 1120, 1875 Connecticut Avenue, NW, Washington, DC 20009.

This report, published every two years, presents information on the broad economic picture of a cross-section of the population aged 55 or older. The tabulations focus on the major sources and combinations of sources of income for this age group, with special emphasis on some aspects of the income of the population aged 65 or older, and the amounts received from such sources. This economic analysis is designed to be of interest to policymakers, researchers, retirement planners, marketers, and actuaries.

Inlander, Charles B. *Medicare Made Easy.* A People's Medical Society book. Reading, MA: Addison-Wesley, 1989. 336p. $10.95, paper. ISBN 0-201-17269-0.

This book is to be used as a reference and a tool to cut through the jargon of the Medicare program and the bureaucratic red tape. It explains every Medicare form and shows the reader how to fill them out, provides sample letters to doctors about fees and coverage, shows how to file a claim, and explains the patient's rights in a hospital. There are lists of state insurance offices, state nursing home licensure agencies, and state peer review organizations and a glossary. The People's Medical Society, a large consumer-health advocacy organization, has provided a book that will help medical consumers get the most from the health care system.

Matthews, Joseph L. *Social Security, Medicare and Pensions: A Sourcebook for Older Americans.* 3rd ed. Berkeley, CA: Nolo Press, 1990. 240p. $15.95. ISBN 0-87337-096-7.

This sourcebook provides specific answers in plain language to the questions regarding benefit programs available to persons age 55 or over. It explains Social Security retirement and disability benefits, Civil Service and Veterans Administration benefits, private pensions and retirement plans, Medicare, Medicaid and private health insurance, and age discrimination. This comprehensive guide will help those at or near retirement age through the maze of income and benefit programs available to them.

Medicare and Medicaid Data Book. Annual. $4.75. Health Care Financing Administration, ORD Publications, 6325 Security Boulevard, Baltimore, MD 21207.

Published annually as a part of the series *Health Care Financing Program Statistics,* this data book is an overview of the Medicare and Medicaid programs. It provides current basic data and analyses of the programs for use by policymakers, program managers, health planners, and researchers. Subjects include program eligibility, participation, services covered and used, and payments and reimbursements for various periods from 1966 to the present. Appendices include addresses of Medicare carriers; provider information, telephone numbers, and office addresses; a glossary; and a list of acronyms.

On the Other Side of Easy Street: Myths and Facts about the Economics of Old Age. Washington, DC: Villers Foundation, 1987. 66p. Single copy free; additional copies $5. ISBN 0-9617893-0-1.

This report expands on two stereotypes of older Americans—one that sees them as uniformly poor and helpless and a new stereotype that sees them as rich and greedy. In their study of the economics of old age, the foundation presents data and analyses showing that neither stereotype is accurate. They contend that these inaccurate stereotypes lead to conflict between the old and the young at a time when the nation's attention should be on economic security for everyone, regardless of age. This book is often cited in discussions of generational conflict.

Ostroff, Jeff. *Successful Marketing to the 50+ Consumer.* Englewood Cliffs, NJ: Prentice-Hall, 1989. 352p. $59.95. ISBN 0-13-860271-9.

Focused on today's explosive senior market, this resource book provides a host of definitive strategies, practical guidelines, and case studies on how to reach senior consumers. It discusses market trends, consumer needs, fundamentals of advertising and promotion, communication channels, outstanding business opportunities, and future needs. This should be of interest to hospitals, retail businesses, consultants, and libraries—anyone trying to attract the older consumer.

Schultz, James H. *The Economics of Aging.* 4th ed. Dover, MA: Auburn House, 1988. 200p. $29.95. ISBN 0-86569-174-6.

Revised and updated, this is a standard work offering a concise, nontechnical view of the economic status of the elderly. This edition also gives greater coverage of key issues such as expenditures for elderly programs, changes in the Social Security law, retirement income planning, the role of employer-sponsored pensions, and economic security today and tomorrow. This comprehensive study will help social policy planners as well as those working with older individuals.

Shane, Dorlene V., and the United Seniors Health Cooperative. *Finances after 50.* New York: Harper & Row, 1989. 206p. $10.95. ISBN 0-06-096231-3.

This practical, self-study guide and workbook aims to help those over 50 organize and plan their financial future. The author, a certified financial planner, provides worksheets and information to help the reader create a personalized financial plan. By considering income and expenses, health, life and property insurance, taxes, and investments, the reader will get information he or she needs to chart a financial plan.

Thomas, William W., ed. *All about Medicare.* 3rd ed. Chicago, IL: National Underwriter Co. and Probus Publishing Co., 1990. 79p. $6.95. ISBN 0-87218-471-4.

———, ed. *Social Security Manual.* 30th ed. Chicago, IL: National Underwriter and Probus Publishing Co., 1990. 209p. $9.95. ISBN 0-87218-470-6.

Each of these pocket-size books is an indispensable guide for the professional working with this information and for the senior consumer. Each contains the most up-to-date laws in their respective areas. *All about Medicare* covers both parts A and B of the program, prescription drugs, and submission of claims/appeals. Appendices include a table of Medicare benefits and addresses for submitting claims. The *Social Security Manual* explains how benefits are calculated, taxation and loss of benefits, and how to file for benefits and includes tables of benefit levels.

U.S. Department of Health and Human Services, Social Security Administration. *Social Security Handbook*. Annual. Washington, DC: Superintendent of Documents. $13. Stock No. 017-070-00420-2.

This handbook is intended for people who want an explanation of federal retirement programs, survivors disability benefits, black lung benefits, Supplemental Security Income (SSI) programs, and health insurance so that they may understand how these programs operate, who is entitled to benefits, and how these benefits may be obtained. It is for sale by the Government Printing Office and may also be examined or copied at any Social Security office.

Where Coverage Ends: Catastrophic Illness and Long-Term Health Care Costs. Washington, DC: Employee Benefit Research Institute, 1988. 274p. $19.95. ISBN 0-86643-061-X.

In this book, the Employee Benefit Research Institute brings together experts from the health care field, academia, government, and labor to assess catastrophic health care needs in the United States and how to finance them. The book examines in detail how we define catastrophic costs and who is at risk of incurring them, what roles the private insurance market and the federal government currently play and their effectiveness, and how our society should finance catastrophic medical and long-term care expenses. This book should be read by a wide audience, since everyone is at risk of incurring major medical expenses or needing long-term care.

PERIODICALS

Health Care Financing Review. 4/yr. $15. Health Care Financing Administration, 2E6 Oak Meadows Building, 6325 Security Boulevard, Baltimore, MD 21207.

This quarterly journal contains data on national health expenditures, the percentage of those expenditures covered by Medicare, and other topics on utilization of health care.

Medicare and Medicaid Data Book. Annual. $4.75. Health Care Financing Administration, ORD Publications, 6325 Security Boulevard, Baltimore, MD 21207.

This annual report presents data on Medicare and Medicaid program eligibility, participation, covered services and their usage, and payments and reimbursements.

Social Security Bulletin. 12/yr. $16. Superintendent of Documents, U.S. Government Printing Office, Washington, DC 20402-9325.

This journal focuses on the activities of the Social Security Administration. Articles report on aspects of the Social Security service, news of program operations, and summaries of recent research, and monthly tables of current operating statistics are included. The general public, older adults, and specialists in aging will need this publication to keep abreast of the changes, policies, and directives within this huge agency.

Social Security Bulletin Annual Statistical Supplement. Annual. $16. Included in a subscription to the *Social Security Bulletin,* or may be ordered separately. Stock No. 717-026-00000-4. Superintendent of Documents, U.S. Government Printing Office, Washington, DC 20402-9325.

This data-packed compilation is one of the most widely used references in the field of social insurance and social welfare. It features the latest comprehensive data on Social Security retirement and disability benefits, Medicare and Medicaid, and other programs such as unemployment insurance, veterans' benefits, and income-supported programs (such as Supplemental Security Income, or SSI, and food stamps). Detailed tables are preceded by a concise legislative history of each of the major programs. This publication is a worthwhile addition to all collections on aging.

AUDIOVISUAL RESOURCE

Due upon Receipt
Type: Slides/audiotape
Length: 19 min.
Date: 1987

Cost: $67.50
Source: Vicki Schmall
Oregon State University Extension Service
Milam 161
Corvallis, OR 97331-5106

This program addresses the financial concerns of the elderly by looking at three families. Through Isabel, viewers learn about the problems low-income elderly face and the resources available. Carlos has duplicate health insurance coverage and is a prime target for sales agents. When Maggie is widowed she faces major financial discussions but knows little about her financial situation. Guidelines are presented for making financial decisions in later life in this excellent program for seniors, families, and general community education.

Education: Gerontology and Adult

BOOKS

Elderhostel Catalog. 3/yr. Free. Elderhostel, 80 Boylston Street, Suite 400, Boston, MA 02116.

Produced in the format of a tabloid newspaper, this is a catalog of Elderhostel programs and courses. These courses for older people take place on college campuses in every state and in many Canadian provinces as well as some overseas locations. Only people over 60 or couples, one of whom is over 60, are eligible, and there is a reasonable fee. There are many Elderhostel fans among older adults, and the catalog will help them locate new programs.

Hyman, Mildred. *Elderhostels: The Students' Choice.* Santa Fe, NM: Muir, 1989. 259p. $12.95. ISBN 0-945465-28-9.

This reference is specifically intended for use by students over 60 years of age who are interested in taking college courses through the Elderhostel program. The courses themselves are described in the Elderhostel catalogs. This volume gives detailed descriptions of the quality of the housing, instructors, food available, and covers the difficulties and shortcomings of each program as well. This is an excellent companion to the Elderhostel catalogs.

Peterson, David A. *Career Paths in the Field of Aging.* Lexington, MA: Lexington Books, 1987. 128p. $21; $10.95, paper. ISBN 0-669-15282-X; 0-669-15283-8, paper.

Professional gerontology is a rapidly growing field that offers bright prospects for its practitioners. Written by the dean of the Leonard Davis School of Gerontology at the Andrus Gerontology Center, this study surveys the range of jobs and the opportunities available in the profession. Students and professionals seeking to plan their careers in this burgeoning field will find this a useful guide.

―――――. *Facilitating Education for Older Learners.* San Francisco, CA: Jossey-Bass, 1983. 342p. $21.95. ISBN 0-87589-565-4.

The author strongly believes that adults at every age have the potential to grow and contribute and that education can help adults reach this potential. He summarizes research, both classic and current, on learning ability, intelligence in later life, motivation, learning styles, and teaching methods. He looks at changes and trends in the field of adult education and, though the focus is on older learners, a good general summary of adult education and adult learners in the United States is included. This is a useful text for courses specifically about educational programs for older adults and for courses about adult education. It is also a good program development guide, providing practical information about both teaching and learning.

PERIODICALS

Educational Gerontology: An International Bimonthly Journal. Bimonthly. $45, individuals. $95, institutions. Hemisphere Publishing Corp., 79 Madison Avenue, Suite 1110, New York, NY 10016-7892.

The articles in this journal, written by educators from around the world, are about older adults and their learning habits and abilities. There are papers on topics such as a geriatric curriculum for home health aides and senior citizens as educational resources. The journal includes both book and audiovisual media reviews and would be used by academics, specialists in older adult education, and older adults themselves.

Gerontology & Geriatrics Education. 4/yr. $32, individuals. $42, institutions. $75, libraries. Haworth Press, 10 Alice Street, Binghamton, NY 13904.

This journal is directed to students, educators, practitioners, and others interested or involved in teaching those who work with the elderly, in addition to those educators who teach the elderly themselves. Articles are related to gerontological and geriatric courses and to curriculum design and implementation. There are book reviews, selected conference reports and papers, and articles on innovative programs.

Elder Abuse, Crime Prevention, and Safety

BOOKS

Aday, Ron H. *Crime and the Elderly: An Annotated Bibliography*. Westport, CT: Greenwood Press, 1988. 134p. $35.95. ISBN 0-313-25470-2.

This book contains references published since 1970 in the fields of gerontology, criminology, criminal justice, sociology, and psychology that relate to the victimization of the elderly and their participation in crime. It contains over 360 annotations in three broad categories: crimes against the elderly, the elderly as criminals, and resources and information. Citations include books, journal articles, conference proceedings and papers, research reports, congressional hearings, crime prevention models, and training programs. This book is intended for human services and criminal justice professionals as well as researchers, students, and attorneys working in this field.

Douglass, Richard L. *Domestic Mistreatment of the Elderly—Towards Prevention*. Washington, DC: American Association of Retired Persons, 1987. 39p. Free. No ISBN.

This booklet explores the issue of the mistreatment or neglect of elderly people within the home. It examines what is known about mistreatment of the elderly—the categories of mistreatment, the forms it takes, and its prevalence and severity—and explores what can be done about it. The solution lies both in intervention via current laws and policies and in the long-range solution of prevention by the individual, the family, and the community. This publication will increase public awareness of the issue and, it is hoped, prevent further victimization.

Johnson, Tanya F., et al. *Elder Neglect and Abuse: An Annotated Bibliography*. Westport, CT: Greenwood Press, 1985. 223p. $40.95. ISBN 0-313-24589-4.

Elder Abuse, Crime Prevention, and Safety

This annotated bibliography focuses on maltreatment of the elderly in family settings and brings together selected information on materials written since 1975. The extensive annotated bibliography is followed by an unannotated listing of information pertaining to both family and nonfamily settings. Also included in the publication is a directory of organizations, services, and individuals concerned with aging whose programs may impact on abuse of the elderly. An appendix gives the full text of the Model Adult Protective Services Act.

Persico, J. E., with George Sunderland. *Keeping Out of Crime's Way: The Practical Guide for People over 50.* Washington, DC: American Association of Retired Persons and Scott, Foresman, 1987. 158p. $6.95. ISBN 0-673-24801-1.

Keeping Out of Crime's Way shows the reader how to sharply reduce or eliminate the chance of becoming a crime victim. Simple steps and inexpensive safeguards that can foil a criminal or prevent an emotionally debilitating incident are described. The book includes security checklists and dos and don'ts for coping with many crime situations. This excellent guide to crime prevention, though it is aimed at people over 50, will be useful to all age groups.

Quinn, Mary J., and Susan K. Tomita. *Elder Abuse and Neglect: Causes, Diagnosis and Intervention Strategies.* Vol. 8 of the Springer Series on Social Work. New York: Springer, 1986. 322p. $28.95. ISBN 0-8261-5120-5.

This comprehensive book explores the nature of elder abuse, examines why and how older adults are abused, and provides guidelines for detection and appropriate intervention. The authors discuss many forms of abuse, including physical, psychological, and financial, using case examples from their clinical experience. Detailed protocols for identification and assessment of elder abuse and neglect are included. This book will prove useful to anyone concerned with elder abuse—social workers, scholars, legislators, caregivers, and ordinary citizens.

PERIODICAL

Journal of Elder Abuse and Neglect. 4/yr. $24, individuals; $32, institutions; $42, libraries. Haword Press, 10 Alice Street, Binghamton, NY 13904.

The National Committee for the Prevention of Elder Abuse has designated this journal to be its official publication. It is devoted to the study of the causes, treatment, effects, and prevention of abuse and neglect of older and disabled persons; to the promotion of awareness of the problem; and to the discussion of effective public policies and attitudes.

Employment

BOOKS AND GOVERNMENT PUBLICATIONS

Birren, James E., et al., eds. *Age, Health, and Employment.* Englewood Cliffs, NJ: Prentice-Hall, 1986. 192p. $43.33. ISBN 0-13-018524-8-01.

This book deals with the technological developments in the nature of work, increased longevity, early retirement trends, and concern with productivity. The contributors focus on functional age versus chronological age, age-related health factors in job performance, training older workers, and age as a factor in coping with stress. Of interest primarily to scholars and researchers, this book reviews existing studies and makes specific recommendations for future research.

Bureau of National Affairs. *Older Americans in the Workforce.* Rockville, MD: Bureau of National Affairs, 1987. 237p. $75. ISBN 0-87179-900-6.

This report examines how the aging of the population will affect the workplace and how employers, government, and the older employees themselves will adapt. How will workers plan for retirement and how will employers help prepare them? Who will pay retirees' health care costs? What might it cost employers to keep older workers on the job? This report uses case studies to illustrate how some companies and organizations are dealing with these questions. Employers, unions, governments, attorneys, and associations facing the challenge of adapting to the aging workforce will find the information in this report very useful. There is also a resource guide and extensive bibliography.

Commitment to an Aging Workforce: Strategies and Models for Helping Older Workers Achieve Full Potential. Washington, DC: National Council on the Aging, 1988. 194p. $15. ISBN 0-910883-46-7.

This informative and comprehensive resource manual draws from several sources including cooperative ventures between the National Council on Aging's Prime Time Productivity Program and personnel at six demonstration sites. Close attention is given to ways of improving linkages between the Job Training Partnership Act and other employment-related programs. One section is devoted to program coordination strategies at the state and local levels. Other sections deal with older worker recruitment and training issues and with effective employer outreach strategies. Employers and human resource staff will find the ideas and techniques presented here very helpful.

Dennis, Helen, ed. *Fourteen Steps in Managing an Aging Work Force.* Lexington, MA: Lexington Books, 1988. 272p. $29.95. ISBN 0-669-13206-3.

Contributors from gerontology, business, law, medicine, psychology, sociology, public administration, and social work address the topic of managing the aging workforce. The book is based on the premise that age issues must be addressed while individuals are still employed so that employers can continue to get the best performance from older workers and so that older workers can attain a high level of job satisfaction. The information in this overview can be used by employers, retirement specialists, human resource directors, trainers, and educators.

How To Manage Older Workers. Washington, DC: American Association of Retired Persons, Worker Equity Department, 1988. 16p. Free. No ISBN.

This brief booklet addresses the fact that the nation's population is aging, resulting in a growing number of middle-aged and older employees. The Worker Equity Department of the American Association of Retired Persons (AARP) sees this as a challenge to management and presents strategies to motivate older workers, addresses the influence of age stereotypes on work relationships, and provides tips on managing the older worker.

How To Recruit Older Workers. Washington, DC: American Association of Retired Persons, Worker Equity Department, 1988. 16p. Free. No ISBN.

This booklet is designed to help employers successfully recruit older workers. It describes various groups of older workers and what motivates them. It suggests ways to analyze and modify jobs, benefits, and work environments to make them more attractive to older workers, and it outlines strategies for reaching older persons and recruiting them. This is an excellent resource for employers who are looking beyond their traditional sources of personnel.

How To Train Older Workers. Washington, DC: American Association of Retired Persons, Worker Equity Department, 1988. 16p. Free. No ISBN.

The average age of the workforce is increasing. As a result, much of tomorrow's training will have to be aimed at developing, preserving, and renewing the skills and talents of middle-aged and older workers. This booklet addresses such concerns as the flexibility and capacity of employees to learn new skills, the best way to identify employees who need training and help with career development, and the cost-effectiveness of training and employee development. *How To Train Older Workers* is a practical guide to help employers develop ways to train mid-career and older employees so they can continue to work at peak capacity.

Levin, Robert C. *Wellness Programs for Older Workers and Retirees.* Washington, DC: Washington Business Group on Health, 1987. 63p. $6. No ISBN.

Worksite health promotion programs for older workers and retirees are not plentiful, but some are being offered. This report presents examples of the programs that do exist, focusing on the creative efforts some companies are making to address the area of health promotion for older workers and retirees.

Merrill, Fred L. *Job Search Manual for Mature Workers.* Los Angeles, CA: Los Angeles Council on Careers for Older Americans, 1987. Np. $15. No ISBN.

Written primarily for older job seekers with professional, managerial, and technical backgrounds, this manual can be used in a classroom setting or on a one-to-one basis by a job counselor. Among its many valuable features are checklists, worksheets, and guidelines designed to help older job seekers identify their own needs, strengths, interests, and employment goals. It also offers sample letters and a system for tracking each step in the job hunt.

Polich, Cynthia L., Laura Iverson, and Charles Oberg. *Who Will Pay? The Employer's Role in Financing Health Care for the Elderly.* Excelsior, MN: Interstudy, 1987. 26p. $20. No ISBN.

The purpose of this report is to examine the current and potential roles of employers in financing health care and long-term care benefits for retirees and older workers. Included are discussions of retiree health benefit plans, trends in older workers' benefits and their consequences, and employers' attempts to control costs and, in conclusion, a series of recommendations for the appropriate role of employers in this area. Employers, policymakers, and human resource managers will use this report.

Workers over 50: Old Myths, New Realities. Washington, DC: American Association of Retired Persons, 1986. Np. Free. Stock No. D12429.

This report provides the results of a 1985 Yankelovich, Skelly, and White survey of 400 companies, including policies, practices, programs, and perceptions regarding workers age 50 or over. Two major findings were: 1) most companies value their older employees, and 2) employers' experiences discredit negative stereotypes about older workers. The report offers practical guidance for building business support systems for employment programs for older workers.

Yolles, Stanley, et al., eds. *The Aging Employee.* Vol. 8 of Problems of Industrial Psychiatric Medicine Series. New York: Human Sciences Press, 1984. 173p. $29.95. ISBN 0-89885-106-8.

The contributors to this volume explore common problems and needs of older workers, discussing medical and psychological problems, social networks, utilization of early retirement, and roles played by government, labor, and management. They offer suggestions for improving the conditions of aging workers, knowing their numbers will increase in years to come. This work is valuable to all professionals, managers, and workers who are concerned with the well-being of aging workers.

PERIODICAL

Working Age. 6/yr. Free. American Association of Retired Persons, Worker Equity Department, 1909 K Street, NW, Washington, DC 20048.

This bimonthly publication covers the latest employment facts and demographic trends affecting employees age 50 or over. The information is especially pertinent to employers with older employees as well as to benefits, pension, and personnel directors; specialists in aging; and policymakers.

VIDEOCASSETTE

Partners in Change
Type: ½" VHS videocassette, color
Length: 18 min.

Date: 1989
Cost: $20; free to AARP chapters
Source: AARP Program Resources Department
Station DG
1909 K Street, NW
Washington, DC 20049

This video is designed to increase employer awareness of the problems of displaced homemakers—women who have lost their main source of income through divorce, separation, widowhood, or the job loss of a spouse. Many of these women attempt to enter or re-enter the workforce and face negative stereotypes, low salaries, and a general reluctance to hire older workers. Narrated by Edwin Newman, the videotape features four women who entered the workforce at an older age. Two company executives also discuss how hiring older women has been good for their businesses.

Ethics and Legal Issues

BOOKS

Brown, Robert N. *The Rights of Older Persons.* Carbondale, IL: Southern Illinois University Press, 1989. 413p. $8.95. ISBN 0-8093-1432-0.

Using a question-and-answer format, this guide (one in a series of American Civil Liberties Union, or ACLU, citizens' rights handbooks) concentrates on laws designed to protect the elderly. Among the topics are the right to freedom from restraints on life, liberty, and property and the right to health care. The book also includes a chapter titled "The Right to Refuse Medical Treatment." A list of national and state groups to which both legal and general questions can be referred adds to the value of this reference.

Callahan, Daniel. *Setting Limits.* New York: Simon and Schuster, 1987. 256p. $18.95; $8.95, paper. ISBN 0-671-22477-8; 0-671-66831-5, paper.

Callahan examines the proper goals of medicine in our rapidly aging society where limited biomedical resources are causing a health care crisis. He argues that a disproportionate share of our health care resources are spent on extending the lives of the elderly, with little thought for the quality of these lives. Callahan proposes shifting attention to the relief of suffering and limiting care that is merely life-extending. This controversial view has sparked debate on questions involving the "natural" lifespan, rationing of health care among the generations, and the responsibility of caring for the aged. This is an essential book for anyone interested in medical ethics.

Kapp, Marshall B. *Legal Aspects of Health Care for the Elderly: An Annotated Bibliography.* Westport, CT: Greenwood Press, 1988. 166p. $39.95. ISBN 0-313-26159-8.

This bibliography is designed to help practicing health, human services, and legal professionals identify information sources that will provide essential guidance on the legal implications of health care for the elderly. The book contains more than 600 annotated references covering such subjects as general sources on law, health care, and aging; informed consent; involuntary commitment; protective services; resuscitation; and research involving older human subjects. Citations consist of books, journal articles, and reports published from 1980 on.

Kapp, Marshall B., et al., eds. *Legal and Ethical Aspects of Health Care for the Elderly.* Ann Arbor, MI: Health Administration Press, 1985. 322p. $28. ISBN 0-910701-04-0.

The contributors address issues of financing long-term care; legal issues, such as malpractice and quality control in long-term care; the rights of the older consumer in a long-term care facility; protective services; and informed consent. There is no prevailing philosophical orientation and no answers are provided in this book, but it will give professionals involved either in policymaking for or in direct provision of health care to the elderly a starting point in any discussion of these issues.

Regan, John L. *Your Legal Rights in Later Life.* Washington, DC: American Association of Retired Persons and Scott, Foresman, 1989. 324p. $13.95. ISBN 0-673-24884-4.

A specialist in law on the aged and aging, Regan carefully details how rights and interests can best be protected with some simple legal procedures as we age. The areas covered include income, federal income tax, credit, health care, home ownership, incapacitation, estate planning, and wills/probate. The book is well organized with charts, sample forms, and examples.

Waymack, Mark H., and George A. Taylor. *Medical Ethics and the Elderly: A Case Book.* Chicago, IL: Pluribus Press, 1988. 205p. $29.95. ISBN 0-944496-01-6.

This book fills a specific gap in the medical ethics literature—care of the elderly. The authors do not regard the old as a homogeneous group, but instead suggest that being old makes one different and then pose the question whether these differences should count in ethical decisions. Each chapter opens with a case study, followed by discussion of issues, clinical factors, and ethical positions. The authors present their own position on each issue, but they also discuss alternative views. The book is an excellent medical ethics text and would be useful for any professional group.

Geriatrics

BOOKS AND GOVERNMENT PUBLICATIONS

Brody, Stanley J., and George E. Ruff, eds. *Aging and Rehabilitation.* New York: Springer, 1986. 378p. $38.95. ISBN 0-8261-5360-7.

The numbers of disabled elderly are increasing and challenging the prevailing emphasis on vocational rehabilitation. The contributors to this volume suggest that the goal of geriatric rehabilitation should be in terms of restoring the functions significant to the quality of life and that rehabilitation should be an integral part of the services delivery system for the elderly. Professionals in rehabilitation as well as all members of the medical profession will find this collection of papers informative.

Burnside, Irene. *Nursing and the Aged: A Self-Care Approach.* 3rd ed. St. Louis, MO: McGraw-Hill, 1988. 960p. $39.95. ISBN 0-07-009214-1.

This third edition of Burnside's book has a new format, a new focus, and new material. The chapters cover a general introduction to gerontology, nursing actions—process and human responses, mental health, special needs, environment, and health promotion and nursing research. Pictures, poems, and quotations to stimulate discussion are included at the beginning of each chapter. The book can be used in any sequence because each chapter is designed to stand alone. Most chapters suggest student projects and all are followed by study questions. This is an excellent text for beginning graduate-level nursing students as well as for inservice and continuing education.

Calkins, E., P. J. Davis, and A. B. Ford, eds. *The Practice of Geriatrics.* Philadelphia, PA: W. B. Saunders, 1986. 617p. $75. ISBN 0-7216-2329-8.

This book is designed to be used as a standard text for clinicians involved in the care of elderly patients. Aimed at physicians trained in family practice or internal medicine for whom the aged constitute an increasing proportion of their practice, this book contains practical information regarding psychiatry, urology, ophthalmology, dermatology, dentistry, otolaryngology, and anesthesiology. Most chapters are organized into sections dealing with the presentation of disorders and problems of the aged, followed by treatment recommendations. This is a practical book that can be used as a basic text and as a reference source for the practice of geriatrics.

Crow, Marjorie R. *Pharmacology for the Elderly: The Nurse's Guide to Quality Care.* New York: Teachers College Press, 1984. 147p. $16.95. ISBN 0-8077-2752-0.

All nurses who work or plan to work with elderly patients need to update their knowledge of drug therapy. This text is written specifically for nurses and focuses on drug utilization as it is modified by the aging process. Chapters address such concerns as adverse reactions, techniques of drug administration, and drug interactions. The appendices include such things as a chart presenting adverse drug reactions and selected nursing phrases translated into Spanish and French.

Cusack, Odean, and Elaine Smith. *Pets and the Elderly: The Therapeutic Bond.* New York: Haworth Press, 1984. 257p. $29.95. ISBN 0-86656-259-1.

Increasing research in the field of the human/animal bond is generating evidence that animals make people happier, healthier, and more sociable. This book reports on specific program ideas for communities and for long-term care facilities, presents plans for organizing such programs, and lists organizations involved in pet therapy. Community groups and activity directors considering such a program will find practical information in this book.

Dreher, Barbara. *Communication Skills for Working with Elders.* Vol. 17 of Springer Series on Adulthood and Aging. New York: Springer, 1987. 141p. $17.95. ISBN 0-8261-5620-7.

The goal of this book is to break through the silence barrier that often surrounds the elderly and thereby enhance their well-being. The barriers may be physical, social, or emotional, and readers will discover how illness, changes in dependency or status, and lowered self-esteem can affect communication. The communication information plus the exercises and activities designed to help improve skills in communicating with elderly people make this book practical for therapists, social workers, activity directors, medical personnel, and any other health or helping professional working with the elderly.

Ebersole, Priscilla, and Patricia Hess. *Toward Healthy Aging: Human Needs and Nursing Responses.* 3rd ed. St. Louis, MO: C. V. Mosby, 1989. 800p. $41.95. ISBN 0-8016-2869-9.

This textbook on care of the aged focuses on maintaining and promoting health in the elderly client. The framework for the book is Maslow's hierarchy of needs, emphasizing care of the elderly in the community setting; therefore, importance is placed on interventions that will assist the elderly to remain in the community. The first section of the book details the history, roles, and functions of geriatric nursing and part two is devoted to the needs of older persons. The appendices contain useful assessment tools and information on where to seek additional assistance in the form of pamphlets, audiovisuals, and organizations. The textbook is comprehensive and easy to read, making it useful to students, professional nurses, and families caring for the elderly in the community.

Gallo, Joseph, et al., eds. *Handbook of Geriatric Assessment.* Rockville, MD: Aspen Publishers, Inc., 1988. 231p. $29.50. ISBN 0-87189-781-4.

The intent of this book is to encourage a comprehensive, multidimensional assessment of the geriatric patient. In the clinical evaluation of the elderly patient, the mental, functional, social, values, and economic spheres cannot be neglected, and this handbook presents relevant questionnaires and other assessment materials that can be used in clinical settings. Physicians, social workers, and nurses will find this book helpful in treating the geriatric patient in various situations, including placement, evaluation of confusion, or multiple medical problems.

Haug, Marie R., ed. *Elderly Patients and Their Doctors.* New York: Springer, 1981. 219p. OP; $24,95, paper. ISBN 0-8261-3570-6; 0-8261-3571-4, paper.

This book makes a strong case for modifications in medical education as a precondition for improvements in the practice of medical care for the elderly. Considering the large growth of the numbers of elderly, the complexities of disease and old age have not yet been appreciated fully by medical and other health schools. Since the older person's condition is usually chronic and long term, the authors call for patient-doctor relationships that recognize a multidisciplinary approach to getting the elderly patient all the services he or she needs.

Kane, Rosalie A., and Robert L. Kane. *Assessing the Elderly: A Practical Guide to Measurement.* Lexington, MA: Lexington Books, 1981. 320p. $29; $16, paper. ISBN 0-669-04551-9; 0-669-09780-2, paper.

Providers of long-term care services to the elderly will find this a logically organized volume containing explanations, evaluations, and comparisons of the most common measurement tools used to assess the physical, mental, social, and multidimensional functioning of elderly clients. The authors' analysis of the tests used to measure physical, mental, and social functions and their discussion of the uses and abuses of geriatric assessment make this book useful for planning purposes as well as for individual assessment.

Reichel, William, ed. *Clinical Aspects of Aging.* 3rd ed. Baltimore, MD: Williams & Wilkins, 1989. 626p. $69.95. ISBN 0-683-07204-8.

This third edition of a durable textbook (first published in 1978) is a manual for the primary care physician. The new edition gives increased space to psychosocial aspects of the care of the elderly and adds a section on medical ethics, thereby placing "a major emphasis on the problems of the elderly patient rather than simply preparing a subspecialty treatise." There are 44 chapters in sections dealing with evaluation, diagnosis and management, "other considerations," and ethical considerations. The book is a standard textbook in the field of geriatric medicine because it dispenses sensible advice from experienced geriatricians that will help primary care physicians in their practices.

A Resource Guide for Nutrition Management Programs for Older Persons. Washington, DC: U.S. Administration on Aging, 1985. Np. $5. ISBN 1-55672-0003-3.

This resource guide was written specifically as an aid in the development of community nutrition management programs for seniors. There are program models and lists of resource materials along with strategies for utilization of community resources. In addition to its use in program development, the material in this guide may be used to train agency staff.

Roe, Daphne A. *Geriatric Nutrition.* 2nd ed. Englewood Cliffs, NJ: Prentice-Hall, 1987. 267p. $34.67. ISBN 0-13-354077-4.

The knowledge base concerning the nutrition needs of those over 65 is still in its infancy. Much of the current nutritional information is based on studies that extrapolate from younger populations or compare the young and the old. This book presents what facts are known and raises issues and questions about future research. In this second edition the chapters on drugs and nutrition in the elderly and assessment of nutritional status have been expanded and a chapter on degenerative diseases in Third World countries has been added. This is a basic textbook for senior and graduate students and a useful reference for professionals.

Saxon, Sue V., and Mary Jean Etten. *Physical Change and Aging: A Guide for the Helping Professions.* 2nd ed. New York: Tiresias Press, 1987. 288p. $11.95, paper. ISBN 0-913292-11-7.

This book focuses on the physical changes and common pathologies associated with normal aging. Neither superficial nor highly technical, it discusses each of the major body systems in terms of normal functioning, normal age-related changes, psychological and social implications of such changes, and, briefly, major age-related disorders and diseases. Those with a limited background in medicine and/or gerontology will find this book ideal. It would be valuable as a training manual for workshops, continuing education courses, and inservice education.

Steffl, Bernita M., ed. *Handbook of Gerontological Nursing.* New York: Van Nostrand Reinhold, 1984. 567p. $43.95. ISBN 0-442-27845-4.

This handbook covers both the research background and the day-to-day procedures required for effective response to the special nursing needs of the elderly. The contributors provide a full overview of the physiological care and physical assessment of older patients. There is also thought-provoking coverage of developmental tasks faced by the elderly, such as learning to live with infirmities and preparing for death. For nurses and nursing students, this handbook offers expert practical advice on gerontological nursing care.

Stroud, Marion, and Evelyn Sutton. *Activities Handbook and Instructor's Guide for Expanding Options for Older Adults with Developmental Disabilities.* Baltimore, MD: Paul H. Brookes Publishing, 1988. 255p. $29, paper. ISBN 0-933716-94-X.

This handbook offers detailed directions for specific, independent activities for older persons plus complete instructional plans for self-testing or inservice staff training. Providing hands-on exercises and 64 task-analyzed activities, the handbook shows professionals how to begin training adults for community participation and how to teach independence skills such as personal grooming, making conversation, cleaning an apartment, and how to find help when it is needed. This is an excellent book on helping older adults with disabilities who are about to be de-institutionalized—a subject on which there is very little information.

Tideiksaar, Rein. *Falling in Old Age: Its Prevention and Treatment.* Vol. 22 of Springer Series on Adulthood and Aging. New York: Springer, 1989. 196p. $24.95. ISBN 0-8261-5290-2.

One of the most significant health care problems for the elderly is that of falling and its consequences. The mainstay of fall management for the older person has been to restrict their activities or place them into physical restraints. The author has developed this program to educate health professionals on the subject of falls—their extent and consequences, the many factors involved, and management techniques for fall prevention. Geriatric practitioners and students of geriatrics will find this text, one of very few written on this subject, extremely valuable.

PERIODICALS

Geriatrics: For the Primary Care Physician. 12/yr. $20. Modern Medicine Publications, 7500 Old Oak Boulevard, Cleveland, OH 44130.

This journal is designed to assist primary care physicians in the care of people over 50. It contains practical advice for physicians based on the specialized knowledge needed for the care of older patients. Articles are in categories such as cardiology or neurology, and there are abstracts of journal articles to update physicians on current geriatric literature.

✓ *Journal of Nutrition for the Elderly.* 4/yr. $32, individuals. $75, institutions. $105, libraries. Haworth Press, 10 Alice Street, Binghamton, NY 13904.

This is the only journal that concentrates on the subject of nutrition for the aging. It is addressed to dietitians, nurses, physicians, and administrators. The journal covers all essential aspects of nutrition and publishes research papers by national and international authors. Some articles focus on the problems of older people in the community, but most concern issues of nutrition in institutions. In addition to the articles, there are book reviews, abstracts of current relevant journal articles, and short items on newsworthy topics in the field.

✓ National Center for Health Statistics. *Advance Data from Vital and Health Statistics.* Irregular. Free. National Center for Health Statistics (NCHS), 3700 East-West Highway, Hyattsville, MD 20782.

This is a continuing series of reports published at irregular intervals containing data from NCHS surveys and collections. The reports are brief—a combination of narrative, charts, and tables—and are a means of early release of data that is important for statisticians and planners. For instance, reports on the continuing National Hospital Discharge Survey and on Diagnosis Related Groups are issued in *Advance Data* because the information is so important to decisions on Medicare.

✓ ———. *Vital and Health Statistics Series.* (Popularly known as the *Rainbow Series.*) Irregular. $1.00–$2.50. National Center for Health Statistics, 3700 East-West Highway, Hyattsville, MD 20782.

This irregular publication appears in 13 separate series, all told. Each of the series, all reporting from ongoing surveys, uses age as one of the important variables. The reports that are of special interest to geriatrics and gerontology are in series 3 (#18—"Geographic patterns and the risk of dying and associated factors ages 35-74 years"); series 13 (#51—"Characteristics of nursing home residents, health status and care received: National Nursing Home Survey, U.S."); and series 14 (#25—"Employees in nursing homes in the U.S.: 1977 Nursing Home Survey"). While these reports may have a limited, special audience, i.e., planners and researchers, the information they contain is absolutely vital to those who need it.

Health

It is not the purpose of this book to suggest a complete health of the aging collection; therefore, the author has included a list of materials covering only the major medical problems of the aging population.

Arthritis and Osteoporosis

BOOKS

Fries, James F. *Arthritis: A Comprehensive Guide to Understanding Your Arthritis.* Reading, MA: Addison-Wesley, 1986. 262p. $9.95. ISBN 0-201-05408-6.

Fries, chief of the Arthritis Clinic at Stanford University, offers a positive program for understanding and coping with arthritis or rheumatism. The book is organized around three steps one can take: identify the kind of arthritis; manage it, through treatments, medications, and tests; and learn to manage everyday problems such as pain and side effects from medication. There is also a reading list of books on arthritis, including both recommended and nonrecommended works.

Gach, Michael R. *Arthritis Relief at Your Fingertips: The Complete Self-Care Guide to Easing Aches and Pains without Drugs.* New York: Warner Books, 1989. 231p. $18.95. ISBN 0-446-51474-8.

The author, an acupressure therapist, presents a holistic combination of massage, gentle stretching, and pressure-point stimulation to increase circulation in and around inflamed joints, restore flexibility, and decrease stress. Though these exercises are not meant to replace traditional medical treatment, they offer relief with no risk and are easily integrated into one's life. Photographs and line drawings make the instructions easy to follow.

Kushner, Irving, ed. *Understanding Arthritis.* New York: Charles Scribner's Sons, 1984. 290p. $18.95. ISBN 0-684-18199-1.

Written by the medical staff of the Arthritis Foundation, *Understanding Arthritis* gives the reader a thorough reference to all aspects of the disease. There are sections on diagnosis and treatment, locating community resources, and the 16 most common forms of arthritis and information on unproven methods and special diets as treatment. This is a practical and accurate resource for every person with arthritis.

Lorig, Kate, and James F. Fries. *The Arthritis Handbook: A Tested Self-Management Program for Coping with Your Arthritis.* Reading, MA: Addison-Wesley, 1986. 266p. $9.95. ISBN 0-201-05468-X.

Based on the highly successful program developed at the Stanford University Arthritis Center, the helpbook contains self-treatment strategies that will help reduce the pain of arthritis. These include exercise, pain management techniques, diet and nutrition, drugs, and coping strategies. Designed as a companion guide to *Arthritis: A Comprehensive Guide*, this program will help arthritis patients apply the factual information in that book to help themselves.

Mayes, Kathleen. *Osteoporosis: Brittle Bones and the Calcium Crisis.* Santa Barbara, CA: Pennant Books, 1986. 176p. $12.95; OP, paper. ISBN 0-915201-14-3; 0-915201-15-1, paper.

Osteoporosis is a sad, deforming, crippling bone disease for which there is no cure, but with a lifelong course of preventive action against osteoporosis, women can avoid this suffering. The author presents a program of good nutrition and regular daily exercise, stressing intake of calcium-rich foods, that will strengthen bones. She answers such questions as what are the best sources of dietary calcium, what to do if you can't drink milk, how much sunshine you need, and what to do if you already have osteoporosis. There are a glossary of medical terms and a list of the calcium content of common foods. Women will find this a very helpful book for fighting brittle bones.

Moskowitz, Roland W., and Marie R. Haug, eds. *Arthritis and the Elderly.* New York: Springer, 1986. 195p. $21.95. ISBN 0-8261-4710-0.

One phenomenon of the twentieth century is the shift in major health problems from acute to chronic diseases. The elderly are most vulnerable to chronic conditions, of which arthritis is a prime example. The literature on aging and arthritis as a specific problem is limited, so this volume, which presents the social, emotional, and economic implications of the disease along with the biological and medical issues, will prove useful to physicians, therapists, nurses, social workers, and students of our health care system.

Notelovitz, Morris, and Marsha Ware. *Stand Tall! The Informed Woman's Guide to Preventing Osteoporosis.* Gainesville, FL: Triad Publishing Co., 1982. 208p. $12.95; OP, paper. ISBN 0-937-40415-2; 0-937-40414-4, paper.

Stand Tall is geared to young and middle-aged women who wish to prevent osteoporosis as well as to post-menopausal women who need to halt further bone loss. The authors have compiled research results on the preventive benefits of nutrition, exercise, calcium, and hormone replacement therapy. Topics covered include signs of bone loss, tests to determine if you are losing bone, what kind of exercise is best, how to prevent osteoporosis from becoming worse, and how to help your daughter prevent osteoporosis. This is medical information written in lay language for every woman over the age of 30.

Peck, William A., and Louis V. Avioli. *Osteoporosis—The Silent Thief.* An AARP book. Glenview, IL: Scott, Foresman, 1987. 134p. $9.95. ISBN 0-673-24837-2.

Osteoporosis is known as the silent thief—the end result of gradual losses of bone tissue that accompany aging. The authors believe that this serious problem is potentially preventable, and they present information on diagnosing and treating osteoporosis and offer advice on how this condition can be prevented. Written in clear language for the general public.

Cancer

BOOKS

The American Cancer Society Cancer Book: Prevention, Detection, Diagnosis, Treatment, Rehabilitation, Cure. New York: Doubleday, 1986. 650p. $22.50. ISBN 0-385-17847-6.

Many of the country's leading cancer specialists contributed to this highly readable source of cancer information for the layperson. These experts give detailed guidelines and practical advice about specific forms of cancer, methods of prevention, early detection, the doctor-patient-family relationship, and suggestions for living with the disease. There are a glossary, tables, and a listing of cancer research and treatment centers.

The Complete Book of Cancer Prevention: Foods, Lifestyles & Medical Care To Keep You Healthy. Emmaus, PA: Rodale Press, 1988. 562p. $16.95, paper. ISBN 0-87857-874-9.

Divided into four parts, this book names the cancers that result either in part or in whole from lifestyle, offers specific information on prevention, includes recipes using the best cancer-preventing nutrients, and describes the latest in cancer treatments and ways to avoid some of their worst side effects. By the editors of *Prevention* magazine, this book will be valuable for the layperson, who can use the information to understand a doctor's advice and put options into perspective.

Cardiovascular Disease

BOOKS

Cohn, Keith, and Darby Duke. *Coming Back: A Guide to Recovering from Heart Attack.* Rev. ed. Reading, MA: Addison-Wesley, 1987. 228p. $9.95, paper. ISBN 0-201-05498-1.

Coming Back answers questions for heart and coronary patients about what goes on in the hospital, what certain drugs do, tests, equipment, and procedures. It guides the patient through the stages of heart attack and recovery and provides new information on approaches to reducing stress, managing weight, stopping smoking, and getting back to normal with activities such as eating out and shopping. This book is practical and current and includes self-diagnostic questionnaires, charts showing the odds for different kinds of health risks, and illustrations that explain medical concepts.

Dunkle, Ruth E., and James W. Schmidley, eds. *Stroke in the Elderly: New Issues in Diagnosis, Treatment and Rehabilitation.* New York: Springer, 1987. 211p. $26.95 ISBN 0-8261-5430-1.

This book provides information on the most recent scientific and clinical approaches to the care of the older stroke victim within three major categories: risk factors, treatment, and rehabilitation. Those experiencing a stroke can suffer from an array of problems including affective disorders and mood changes as well as cognitive, social, and physical impairment. Because stroke can lead to greater physical and social isolation for large segments of the older population, the chapters in this book detail, for health professionals working with elderly stroke victims, the biomedical and sociobehavioral issues involved in effective care.

Kra, Siegfried. *Coronary Bypass Surgery: Who Needs It?* New York: W. W. Norton, 1987. 253p. $7.95, paper. ISBN 0-393-30449-3.

Is coronary bypass surgery recommended too frequently these days? A cardiologist talks about what the indications are for this procedure and what alternatives are available. Kra answers questions about nonsurgical alternatives, including medication, diet, and exercise. He devotes four chapters to bypass surgery and its risks, benefits, and aftermath. And finally, he discusses the role of pacemakers, transplants, and artificial hearts. The layperson will gain a greater understanding of what coronary artery bypass surgery is all about from this book.

Purcell, Julia, et al. *Heart Attack: What's Ahead?* Atlanta, GA: Pritchett & Hull Associates, 1986. 64p. $3.75. ISBN 0-939838-02-8.

This book is for people who have had a heart attack and for their families. It will tell them what causes a heart attack, how the heart heals, how a heart attack affects their moods and activities, and the risk factors for heart disease. There are exercises, a home walk program, ways to relax, and clues for identifying any future heart attack. Each page has cartoon instructions that help explain the information on the page without detracting from the seriousness of the information and advice given.

Rees, Michael K. *The Complete Guide to Living with High Blood Pressure.* Rev. ed. New York: Prentice-Hall, 1988. 286p. $10.95, paper. ISBN 0-13-159310-2.

First published in 1980, this book has been extensively revised to reflect the revolution in the treatment of high blood pressure. The chapter on the treatment of high blood pressure with medicines has been completely rewritten. Those with high blood pressure and their families will learn about safe exercise techniques, a prudent diet, nonmedical techniques used to control blood pressure, and medications and their side effects.

The Road Ahead: A Stroke Recovery Guide. Englewood, CO: National Stroke Association, 1986. 153p. $14.95. No ISBN.

This book is meant to answer the questions individuals and their families have when a stroke occurs and to provide guideposts during recovery. Included are an explanation of what a stroke is and all its various symptoms, perspectives on coping with problems, and details about the after-effects of a stroke, such as paralysis, speech problems, perceptual difficulties, and depression. Appendices provide information on legal aspects of having a disability and list community and national resources for further information. Common concerns of caregivers are discussed. Families, stroke victims, and health professionals will all find useful information here.

Chronic Illness

BOOKS

Pitzele, Sefra Kobrin. *We Are Not Alone: Learning To Live with Chronic Illness.* New York: Workman Publishing, 1985. 335p. $8.95. ISBN 0-89480-139-2.

About 30 percent of the adult population suffer from one of the major chronic illnesses such as the dystrophies, multiple sclerosis, heart disease, arthritis, and permanent impairment from stroke. Chronic diseases are permanent and require radical changes of lifestyle, goals, and vocation. The author, who is chronically ill, aims to help victims understand the universality of their feelings and to give practical advice for living. There are chapters on family relationships and choosing doctors, strategies for coping with pain and depression, and practical suggestions on caring for and protecting the body. There are lists of organizations for the chronically ill and addresses of suppliers of products and services. This handbook should be both a source of comfort and a guide for daily life for the chronically ill.

Strong, Maggie. *Mainstay: For the Well Spouse of the Chronically Ill.* Boston, MA: Little, Brown, 1988. 323p. $8.95, paper. ISBN 0-14-011978-7.

As a healthy spouse, how do you deal with the devastation of multiple sclerosis, Parkinson's disease, Alzheimer's disease, or any other chronic illness? In this book, Maggie Strong alternates her personal account with chapters of information on the depression, fatigue, isolation, anxiety, and loneliness that can accompany a chronic illness in the family. The well spouse is often overlooked, and *Mainstay* is a reflective as well as practical guide for those who are caring for the chronically ill.

Diabetes

BOOKS

Berg, Kris E. *Diabetic's Guide to Health and Fitness: An Authoritative Approach to Leading an Active Life.* Champaign, IL: Life Enhancement Publications, 1986. 261p. $12.95. ISBN 0-87322-901-0.

In this guide to health and fitness, the author, himself a diabetic, combines personal experiences with his expertise as an exercise physiologist to show

how diabetics can lead an active life. The reader learns how to control blood sugar; how to lose weight and keep it off; how to handle special situations such as illness, travel, holidays, insulin reaction, and dining out; and how to set up a personal fitness program. A good addition to a consumer health collection for seniors or for any age.

Jovanovic, Lois, June Biermann, and Barbara Toohey. *The Diabetic Woman.* Los Angeles, CA: Jeremy P. Tarcher, 1987. 246p. $15.95; $9.95, paper. ISBN 0-87477-410-1; 0-0-87477-411-X, paper.

For women, diabetes compounds the stresses and demands of a career, marriage, and motherhood. It also complicates the physiological processes of puberty, pregnancy, menstruation, and menopause. Lois Jovanovic is a diabetic wife and mother and a specialist in the problems of women diabetics. She answers questions that women diabetics ask concerning problems and decisions related to employment, health care insurance, contraception, whether or not to have children, and other daily living concerns.

Learning To Live Well with Diabetes. Minnetonka, MN: Diabetes Center, Inc., 1987. 394p. $19.95, paper. ISBN 0-937721-08-5.

This book was written for diabetics of all ages, and the elderly will find it extremely useful. There is a general overview of diabetes information and information about insulin therapy and diabetic care for people with Type II (non-insulin-dependent) diabetes, which is usually developed after the age of 40. Special chapters discuss diabetes and eye problems, foot problems, care and maintenance of a diabetic's healthy heart, and exercise. Individuals and their families will find that this book is easy to use and that they can continue to use it for many years.

Little, Billie, and Victor Ettinger. *Gourmet Recipes for Diabetics.* New York: Periges Books, 1987. 223p. $8.95. ISBN 0-399-51279-9.

This book provides diabetics with recipes for main courses, appetizers, soups, salads, desserts, and drinks—all conforming to a diabetic's dietary regime. The recipes are also suitable for nondiabetics who want to lose weight or maintain optimum weight level or who have a heart problem or other disorder for which a doctor has recommended a sensible diet. The authors have included daily menu guides and the American Diabetes Association exchange lists, which will help keep a diabetic's diet flexible and creative.

Drugs

BOOKS

AARP Pharmacy Service Prescription Drug Handbook. Washington, DC: AARP Books, 1988. 1000p. $25; $13.95, paper. ISBN 0-673-24887-9; 0-673-24842-9, paper.

The handbook is arranged by specific medical condition (such as digestive disorders or respiratory problems), with a brief discussion of each condition, its causes and diagnosis, and drugs used in treatment. The handbook also provides generic and brand names for each drug, possible side effects, storage instructions, and special considerations for those over 65. In addition, there is a drug name index and a special 40-page, full-color Drug Identification Chart. Its arrangement by medical condition and its easy-to-understand language make the handbook a valuable reference.

Katcher, Brian S. *Prescription Drugs: An Indispensable Guide for People over 50.* New York: Macmillan, 1988. 357p. $22.50. ISBN 0-689-11915-1.

This book was written by a pharmacist as a drug guide for people in the general population who are over the age of 50. The first part of the book contains a brief description of how drugs are used in the body and some differences in how medicines affect older persons. The second part of the book presents 92 drugs used most frequently by the aged. Medications are listed by both their generic and brand names and listings include possible side effects and interactions with other drugs. The information is concise and up-to-date.

Physician's Desk Reference. Annual. Oradell, NJ: Medical Economics Co. $39.95. ISBN 0-87489-709-2.

PDR gives information regarding prescription drugs according to the manufacturer. It is organized as follows: Manufacturer's Index (name of company) and Commercial name of drug; Product Category Index (name of general type of drug, such as "Thyroid Preparations"); Generic or chemical name index (e.g., "pentacozine hydrochloride"). People ask for this volume by name, and, although it is not as easy to use as the other drug guides listed, it is by far the best known.

Physician's Desk Reference for Nonprescription Drugs. Annual. Oradell, NJ: Medical Economics Co. $28.95. ISBN 0-87489-701-7.

Arranged like the guide to prescription drugs, this volume gives information, as provided by the drug manufacturer, on over-the-counter drugs. As with the companion volume, users will ask for this book by name.

Wolfe, Sidney M., et al. *Worst Pills, Best Pills: The Older Adult's Guide to Avoiding Drug-Induced Death or Illness.* Washington, DC: Public Citizen Health Research Group, 1988. 532p. $12. No ISBN.

This book, printed in large type, is designed to inform the consumer of the risks and benefits of 287 drugs most commonly prescribed to older adults. Written in nontechnical language and in an easy-to-use format, this guide includes a drug worksheet and examples of the types of questions patients should ask their doctors when medication is prescribed.

Incontinence

PERIODICAL

HIP Report. 4/yr. $5. HIP, Inc., P.O. Box 544, Union, SC 29379.

HIP (Help for Incontinent People) was organized in 1983 to assist the estimated 11 million Americans and Canadians who have bladder-control problems. The organization functions as a clearinghouse of information and services, and their newsletter answers questions of a general nature about drugs, exercise, prostate surgery, treatment options for incontinence, and types of incontinence. They also publish a *Resource Guide of Continence Products and Services.* Although not age-specific, this inexpensive newsletter is a helpful and unique addition to a collection on aging that will be appreciated by older consumers, their families, and those who treat the elderly.

Menopause

BOOKS

Cutler, Winnifred B., et al. *Menopause: A Guide for Women and the Men Who Love Them.* New York: W. W. Norton, 1983. 245p. $9.95, paper. ISBN 0-393-30242-3.

This book is designed to help women and men become informed about menopause. Chapters explain what the change of life is, changing sexuality, osteoporosis, hormone replacement therapy, and hysterectomies and their side effects. Written for men and women with no scientific background, this book will answer questions about menopause and will help older women maximize their use of the health care system.

Greenwood, Sadja. *Menopause, Naturally: Preparing for the Second Half of Life.* San Francisco, CA: Volcano Press, 1984. 201p. $11.95. ISBN 0-912078-74-X.

After discussing menopause—the facts about osteoporosis, menopausal bleeding, estrogen replacement therapy, hot flashes, and the diversity of each woman's menopausal experiences—Greenwood devotes the last half of her book to ways of adjusting to these changes. Relaxation, exercise, nutrition, and health care can all be used by every woman, regardless of the complexity of her midlife changes, to promote good health and zest in the "second half of life." The book has recipes and a reading list along with practical information about vitamins, hormones, and exercise guidelines.

Parkinson's Disease

BOOKS

Duvoisin, Roger C. *Parkinson's Disease: A Guide for Patient and Family.* 2nd ed. New York: Raven Press, 1984. 206p. $27.00; 15.50, paper. ISBN 0-89004-904-1; 0-89004-177-6, paper.

Using layperson's terms, Roger Duvoisin discusses the fundamental pathology of Parkinsonism, the symptoms and course of the disease, drug therapies and their side effects, and beneficial exercise and diet. This guide goes into much more detail than those published by the National Association for Parkinson's Disease and will answer many questions the patient might not think to ask the doctor.

Hutton, J. Thomas, and Raye L. Dippel, eds. *Caring for the Parkinson Patient: A Practical Guide.* Buffalo, NY: Prometheus Books, 1989. 196p. $18.95; $13.95, paper. ISBN 0-87975-478-8; 0-87975-562-8, paper.

This comprehensive collection provides information and helpful suggestions for patients, families, and caregivers to aid them as they adjust to one of the nation's most debilitating chronic neurological disorders. The contributors address new research and treatments for Parkinson's disease, nursing care, speech and communication physical therapy, the serious dangers of falls, depression and other psychiatric effects of the disease, and the benefits and importance of community support systems. *Caring for the Parkinson Patient* is authoritative and highly readable.

Lieberman, Abraham N., et al. *Parkinson's Disease Handbook: A Guidebook for Patients and Their Families.* New York: American Parkinson Association, n.d. 37p. Free. No ISBN.

The American Parkinson Association has produced this booklet for Parkinson's patients and their families to explain the characteristics, causes, therapies, and medications of the disease. Included are a list of answers to commonly asked questions, information on support groups and the association, and a glossary of Parkinson's disease terminology.

VIDEOCASSETTES

Adapting Successfully to Parkinson's Disease
Type: ½" VHS videocassette, color
Length: 30 min.
Date: 1983
Cost: Purchase $295, rental $45
Source: Good Samaritan Hospital and Medical Center
          Audiovisual Services
          1015 Northwest 22nd Avenue
          Portland, OR 97210

This videotape details the daily activities of two people who have Parkinson's disease. It shows the array of care and support that families of the patients and the patients themselves can expect from psychologists and a variety of other therapists.

Get Up and Go
Type: ½" VHS videocassette, color
Length: 60 min.
Date: 1986
Cost: $42.95
Source: Health Tapes, Inc.
          P.O. Box 47196
          Oak Park, MI 48237

Professionals in neurology, physical therapy, and rehabilitation have worked together to create this excellent videotape designed for persons with Parkinson's disease. The work focuses on the prevention of contractures and on improvements in endurance and muscle strength. The videotape also attempts to facilitate social interaction among those performing the presented exercise routines.

Rehabilitation

BOOK

Trieschmann, Roberta B. *Aging with a Disability.* New York: Demos Publications, 1987. 148p. $27.95. ISBN 0-939957-01-9.

The field of rehabilitation has grown spectacularly in the last 40 years, and now—the ultimate sign of success in this field—individuals with disabilities are aging. Currently, individuals who have lived with spinal injury, polio, and other disabilities for 30, 40, and 50 years are arriving in physicians' offices with a variety of complaints and changes in function that can catch the health care system—taught to treat the disease as static—by surprise. To document the problems such patients present for treatment, the author conducted one-on-one interviews with people who had been disabled at least 30 years and with their families. Trieschmann concludes that various combinations of psychosocial, biological-organic, and environmental resources are needed to help those for whom the natural process of aging has been superimposed on other impairments. This work will be useful to physicians, psychologists, social workers, teachers, policymakers, and the disabled themselves.

Sensory Change

BOOKS

Aging and Sensory Change: An Annotated Bibliography. Washington, DC: Gerontological Society of America, 1988. 67p. $8.50, members; $12.50, nonmembers. ISBN 0-929596-00-5.

This annotated bibliography presents material on aging and sensory change that has been published since 1970, although some relevant earlier works are also included. Contributors include nurses, therapists, social workers, gerontologists, physicians, and other experts in this field. While vision and hearing are the largest sections, taste, smell, touch, interactive conditions, rehabilitation, technology, and biographical accounts are included. The citations contain useful material for clinicians and researchers as well as for all other professionals working with the elderly.

Becker, Gaylene. *Growing Old in Silence.* Berkeley and Los Angeles, CA: University of California Press, 1980. 148p. $19.95. ISBN 0-520-03900-9.

In this first book-length study of deaf people in old age, Gaylene Becker describes how they adapt to their disability and analyzes its particular implications for growing old. She studied 200 people over 60 who either were born deaf or lost their hearing in the first few years of life. These people formed peer groups in school that carried over into adulthood and later eased the burden of aging for its members through a strong support system that fosters the maintenance of deaf identity. Becker suggests that values that stress group participation and interdependence may ease the process of aging more than those that stress autonomy and individualism. Written from an anthropological perspective, *Growing Old in Silence* will help practitioners who provide services to disabled populations increase their understanding of both aging and disability.

Kapperud, Marla J. *The Aging Eye: A Guide for Nurses.* St. Paul, MN: Minnesota Society for the Prevention of Blindness and Preservation of Hearing, 1983. 55p. $6.95. ISBN 0-9612370-5-8.

Many Americans, mostly those over 65, lose their vision to glaucoma, cataracts, macular degeneration, or other eye diseases. Over 50 percent of the potential visual loss can be prevented, however, if such diseases are diagnosed and treated in the early stages of development. This guide, which (in spite of the title) is easily understood by the layperson, presents information on common age-associated diseases of the eye, provides a condensed look at psychological aspects of aging and blindness, and offers practical tips for helping the blinded adult develop adaptive techniques. This is an excellent manual for an education program for health professionals or people in the community.

Miller, Alfred L. *A Practical Guide to Hearing Aid Usage.* Springfield, IL: Charles Thomas, 1988. 74p. $21.75. ISBN 0-398-05430-4.

This guide was developed in response to incomplete information in manufacturers' instruction manuals on hearing aids and hearing-aid usage. Miller presents the facts on what a hearing aid can and cannot do for hearing loss. He identifies the most common problems associated with hearing-aid usage and provides answers to questions about different types of hearing aids, causes of hearing loss, and evaluating and choosing a hearing device. This is a useful reference for hearing-aid users and their families as well as for professionals.

Rosenbloom, Alfred A., and Meredith W. Morgan, eds. *Vision and Aging: General and Clinical Perspectives.* New York: Professional Press, 1986. 393p. $60. ISBN 0-87873-045-1.

This book deals with the identification, assessment, and correction of visual disabilities that occur in the older adult. As part of this discussion, it places the technical issues of visual function in the aged within a psychological and social context. The contributors' topics include contact lenses and the elderly patient, the optometric examination of the elderly patient, care in institutional settings, fitting and dispensing spectacles, and aphakia. This book will meet the needs of practitioners and students who need to review and expand their knowledge of the field of vision and aging.

Shulman, Julius. *Cataracts: The Complete Guide—from Diagnosis to Recovery—for Patients and Families.* An AARP book. Des Plaines, IL: Scott, Foresman, 1987. 160p. $7.95. ISBN 0-673-24824-0.

Shulman, an eye surgeon and assistant professor of ophthalmology, presents a detailed yet nontechnical explanation of the workings of the normal human eye. Explaining the many different surgical techniques available, Shulman guides the reader through standard intracapsular and extracapsular lens-removal operations, implants, post-op, and the recovery period. Also included are descriptions of the various types of contact lenses for use after surgery, nonsurgical treatment of cataracts with drugs, and laser cataract surgery.

VIDEOCASSETTES

Look Out for Annie
Type: ½" VHS and Beta videocassette, color
Length: 28 min.
Date: 1987
Cost: ½" VHS $35, ½" Beta $50
Source: National Center for Vision and Aging
111 East 59th Street
New York, NY 10022

This drama explores the problems confronted by older people who lose their sight. It is designed to train and educate health and human services professionals who work with older people. About a widow who has recently lost her sight, the videotape portrays her relationships with family, friends, and the staff of a senior center. The message conveyed is that vision loss for older people need not result in reduced activity or isolation. Annie remains active and involved. A study and discussion guide is included.

When Hearing Fades: Perspectives on Hearing Loss in Later Years
Type: ½" VHS videocassette, color
Length: 60 min.
Date: 1988
Cost: $50
Source: Gallaudet University Press
          800 Florida Avenue, NE
          Washington, DC 20002

When Hearing Fades successfully presents the complex issues concerned with age-related hearing loss. It is basically tutorial, providing an overview of the causes of hearing impairment in adults, the role of hearing aids and assistive listening devices, the psychosocial ramifications of hearing loss, and coping strategies. A manual provides supportive reading material and a list of resource agencies. This is an excellent teaching resource for family members, students, or health professionals.

Home Care

BOOKS

Baulch, Evelyn M. *Extended Health Care at Home: A Complete and Practical Guide.* Rev. ed. Berkeley, CA: Celestial Arts, 1988. 288p. $9.95. ISBN 0-89087-539-9.

With increasing changes in health care and hospitalization, many people are finding that they require long-term health care at home—either by need or by choice. Whether one is recuperating from a traumatic injury, facing a life-threatening illness, or caring for someone who is chronically ill, this book answers questions about finding a nurse or therapist; getting the home ready; pain; and special needs of patients suffering from cancer, Alzheimer's disease, and other conditions. Written from firsthand experience, this book covers both the practical and emotional aspects of home care.

Foyder, Joan Ellen. *Family Caregiver's Guide: The Home Health Care Efficiency System that Really Works.* Cincinnati, OH: Futuro Ohio, 1987. 117p. $14.95. ISBN 0-9617392-0-7.

This book is most appropriate for novice caregivers providing low to moderate amounts of care. It covers personal care, medications, resources for home care, and nutrition, but does not address disabling conditions or care of the terminally ill. It is particularly strong, however, in its focus on advance planning and the psychological aspects of providing care. It discusses emotional reactions to caregiving and what to do to avoid or deal with stress. Those who want general information on what to expect when providing home care will appreciate the sections on how to organize time more efficiently, how to prepare monthly expenses, and how to organize medications and the examples of family agreements.

Friedman, Jo-Ann. *Home Health Care: A Complete Guide for Patients and Their Families.* New York: Fawcett Book Group, 1987. 589p. $14.95. ISBN 0-449-90230-7.

Home Health Care outlines systems, resources, routines, and methods that can make health care at home feasible as an alternative to long-term institutional care. Friedman explains the many potential sources of funding and care and indicates the special services and adjunct therapies that will make the difference in success with home health care. Her goal is to enable the caregiver to coordinate care with others rather than shoulder overwhelming burdens. Approximately half of this book explains the implications of specific diagnoses, including such ailments as cardiovascular problems, respiratory disease, diabetes, Alzheimer's disease, Parkinson's disease, arthritis, and cancer. This coverage in particular will make this volume useful to families of the elderly.

Neidrick, Darla J. *Caring for Your Own: Nursing the Ill at Home.* New York: John Wiley & Sons, 1988. 245p. $12.95. ISBN 0-471-63702-5.

This book is primarily intended for persons providing moderate to high levels of care at home who want practical information on how to deal with daily routines and common problems of home care. The author provides information on medications; bowel and bladder problems; personal care instructions; caring for the terminally ill; and techniques for lifting, changing beds, and modifying the environment. There are detailed instructions for special procedures such as using and administering oxygen and the daily care of catheters, providing extensive coverage not found in all home care books.

Pelham, Anabel O., and William F. Clark, eds. *Managing Home Care for the Elderly: Lessons from Community-Based Agencies.* Vol. 15 of Springer

Series on Adulthood and Aging. New York: Springer, 1986. 196p. $22.95. ISBN 0-8261-4700-3.

Community-based long-term care is relatively new in the United States. It differs from the traditional nursing homes for long-term care in that it attempts to care for frail elders at home. *Managing Home Care for the Elderly* is a collection of essays describing research and demonstration projects recently funded in the United States and Canada. Everyone involved in multidisciplinary team efforts necessary to keeping an elder at home can benefit from the lessons learned in these demonstration projects.

PERIODICALS

Caring. 12/yr. $45. National Association for Home Care, 519 C Street, NE, Washington, DC 20002-5809.

Caring advances the proposition that, as much as is humanly possible, health care and supportive services should be delivered in the home. With that in mind, the magazine publishes articles directed to the home health care and hospice worker or agency director on such topics as quality assurance in home care, education and training, mental health and home care, and aging.

PRIDE Institute Journal of Long Term Home Health Care. 4/yr. $30. Pride Institute, Saint Vincent's Hospital, 153 West 11th Street, New York, NY 10011.

This is the only journal that publishes scholarly articles in the field of long-term home health care. It contains articles that present research, analyze current issues, and report on programs in the long-term home health care field. Subjects can include home intravenous (IV) therapy, home health care services through a health maintenance organization, Medicare outpatient prescription drug benefits, food habits, and home health aides. The journal is addressed primarily to professionals in the home health care field.

Housing, Design, and Environment

BOOKS

The American Institute of Architects (AIA). *Design for Aging: An Architect's Guide.* Washington, DC: The AIA Press, 1985. 179p. $40. ISBN 0-913962-77-5.

Written to be used with current codes and standards, this book is a practical guide to the design issues an architect will face when designing for the needs of the aging. Chapters identify critical site, space, use, and design considerations for five facility types, with a glossary that defines and discusses aging-specific architectural issues. This is a reference work for the practicing architect.

Carlin, Vivian F., and Ruth Mansberg. *If I Live To Be 100: A Creative Housing Solution for Older People.* New York: Princeton Book Co., 1989. Rev. ed. 222p. $12.95, paper. ISBN 0-916622-78-9.

One of the most complicated choices we have to make is where to live when we are old. This guide shows how to make decisions regarding housing and lifestyles during retirement years, with particular emphasis on congregate living. Anyone considering communal housing alternatives will be pleased to see these helpful guidelines on evaluating and choosing a congregate housing lifestyle.

——. *Where Can Mom Live? A Family Guide to Living Arrangements for Elderly Parents.* Lexington, MA: Lexington Books, 1987. 206p. $12.95, paper. ISBN 0-669-13666-2.

More and more people each year face the problem of helping elderly parents find suitable housing arrangements. Carlin and Mansberg show that moving in with the grown children or into nursing homes are not the only options available, and they point out the alternatives: home or apartment sharing, group homes, life-care communities, and, in some cases, staying put. Using actual situations, the authors provide practical information on the psychological, social, and financial consequences of each option. This book will aid families seeking living arrangements for their parents as well as older adults who are looking into changing their housing situation. It includes checklists to evaluate the elder's functional abilities, health, finances, and lifestyle preferences, as well as lists of aging and housing agencies.

Gillespie, Ann E., and Katrinka Smith Sloan. *Housing Options and Services for Older Adults.* Santa Barbara, CA: ABC-CLIO, 1990. 279p. $39.50. ISBN 0-87436-144-3. (In Choices and Challenges: An Older Adult Reference Series.)

This book has been written as a guide for older people, their families, and their advisors, who are investigating various housing and service options.

It is arranged in a very helpful manner with key data about each housing or service option followed by information that answers the questions: What is it? When is it appropriate? How does one find it? and How much does it cost? There is also a consumer checklist for each option that will help the reader in selecting a given service or living arrangement. The authors include a resource section with recommended books and pamphlets and a directory of relevant organizations.

Hochschild, Arlie R. *The Unexpected Community: Portrait of an Old Age Subculture.* Englewood Cliffs, NJ: Prentice-Hall, 1975. 191p. $9.95. ISBN 0-520-03624-7.

This book tells about a community of 43 old people who lived in a small apartment building near the shore of San Francisco Bay. The author, a sociologist, found this community to be a mutual aid society, a source of jobs, a pool of models for growing old, a sanctuary, and a subculture with its own customs, gossip, and humor. This stimulating book about a lower-class housing project is addressed to social scientists, doctors, social workers, the elderly and their families, and planners of public housing. It is often assigned as a textbook in sociology and gerontology courses.

Horne, Jo. *Homesharing and Other Lifestyle Options.* An AARP book. Glenview, IL: Scott, Foresman, 1988. 259p. $12.95. ISBN 0-673-24886-0.

Homesharing and Other Lifestyle Options is about choices in housing. Aimed at seniors, it contains many ideas about alternative living arrangements that can lead to better housing for less money, more security, and new opportunities for companionship. Part one discusses housing options that protect independence such as accessory apartments, group-shared residences, and ECHO (Elder Cottage Housing Opportunities) housing. Often called a Granny Flat, ECHO housing is a free-standing, removable living unit occupied by a relative on the same property as a single-family home. Part two describes housing options with supportive services, including board and care homes, congregate housing, agency-sponsored group-shared residences, and lifecare communities. This well-organized, easy-to-read book is a valuable resource.

Koncelik, Joseph A. *Aging and the Product Environment.* New York: Van Nostrand, 1982. 224p. $36.95. ISBN 0-87933-428-2.

The author makes a case that products created for older people are largely inadequate and do not reflect user characteristics and requirements. He suggests that the continuous process of aging should be matched by products that are designed to meet changes with age. The book gives specific suggestions for designing rooms, furniture, appliances, vehicles, and other products used by the elderly.

Lawton, M. Powell. *Environment and Aging.* 2nd ed. Albany, NY: Center for the Study of Aging, 1986. 205p. $14.95. ISBN 0-937829-00-5.

The first in a planned series of reprints titled *Classics in Aging,* this book's principal contribution is to combine knowledge of environmental sciences and psychology. The built environment sets limits on the behavior of the elderly, but elderly individuals have the ability to adjust to the environment, choosing a course of action from available alternatives. Lawton has added a new chapter to this edition on housing alternatives such as house sharing and group homes. In his new preface, he notes that while we know more about improving the environments of the elderly, the money to do so is increasingly scarce.

Raschko, Bettyann B. *Housing Interiors for the Disabled and Elderly.* New York: Van Nostrand Reinhold, 1982. 350p. $57.95. ISBN 0-442-22001-4.

The author studies the residential needs of the disabled and elderly and answers those needs with viable design strategies. Topics covered include analysis of room design, safety and privacy considerations, furniture designs, silent alarms, and mechanical systems. Designers, architects, and researchers will find help here.

Regnier, Victor, and Jon Pynoos, eds. *Housing the Aged: Design Directives and Policy Considerations.* New York: Elsevier Science Publishing, 1987. 500p. $62.50. ISBN 0-444-01012-2.

The editors have organized the book into three parts: "Planned Housing for the Well Elderly," "Supportive Housing for the Moderately Impaired," and "Housing Environments for the Frail Older Person." Contributors discuss resident satisfaction, social interaction, management, sensory aspects, physiological constraints, and the effect of design on the resident's sense of orientation. Each chapter ends with a section titled "Design Directives and Policy Considerations." This clearly written, well-organized book will serve architects, planners, developers, and gerontologists as a comprehensive reference book.

Sumichrast, Michael, et al. *Planning Your Retirement Housing.* Washington, DC: American Association of Retired Persons, 1987. 259p. $8.95. ISBN 0-673-24810-0.

This guide stresses planning ahead for retirement living and is full of sound advice and practical information on choosing the best retirement housing for any situation, including sections on income, property and sales tax treatment by state, annual average living costs for a retired couple in some 30 locations across the United States, and average day and evening temperatures for more than 200 cities. There are also firsthand comments taken from a group of more than 1,400 people who have shared their retirement experiences—both good and bad—with the authors. Those planning their retirement will find this book helpful as they ponder selling their home, moving to another state, or staying where they are.

AUDIOVISUAL RESOURCES

Coping and Home Safety Tips for Caregivers of the Elderly
Type: ½" VHS videocassette, color
Length: 17 min.
Date: 1987
Cost: Purchase $89.95, rental $10
Source: Jefferson Area Board for Aging
           423 Lexington Avenue
           Charlottesville, VA 22901

As the title implies, this videotape is designed to help family caregivers and home care workers manage the daily activities of older people with chronic physical and mental dysfunction. After brief vignettes showing older people experiencing difficulty lighting a stove, climbing stairs, and buttoning a shirt, the program suggests solutions for these problems. There is a manual that reviews the suggestions in the video, recommends types of community support groups, and lists useful publications. This video is a clear, comprehensible introduction for both laypersons and professionals who are about to have the responsibilities of caregiving.

Designing the Environment for Persons with Dementia
Type: ½" VHS videocassette (color), slides/audiotape
Length: 20 min.
Date: 1989
Cost: ½" VHS $110; slides/audiotape purchase $175, rental $45

Source: Terra Nova Films, Inc.
9848 South Winchester Avenue
Chicago, IL 60643

Focusing on the physical environment, this program suggests ways a properly designed living space can offer support and help compensate for deficits of persons with Alzheimer's disease. Interventions are presented for dealing with disorientation, sensory loss, and spatial problems. A user's manual is included. This is an excellent resource for designers and administrators who are responsible for design considerations.

Intergenerational Relationships

BOOKS

Brubaker, Timothy H., ed. *Family Relationships in Later Life*. Beverly Hills, CA: Sage, 1983. 272p. $35.00; $16.95, paper. ISBN 0-8039-2104-7; 0-8039-2105-5, paper.

Family Relationships in Later Life is a collection of review articles and reports of original research covering topics such as the quality of long-term marriages, intergenerational relationships, role of grandparents in the family, divorce and the elderly, the elderly in minority families, and providing services to older persons and their families. Because it focuses on specific family relationships and specific issues concerning families in later life, the book will appeal to a broad audience, from the researcher to the undergraduate studying gerontology and from policymakers to those actually working with the elderly and their families.

Cherlin, Andrew J., and Frank F. Furstenberg. *The New American Grandparent: A Place in the Family, A Life Apart*. New York: Basic Books, 1988. 288p. $9.95, paper. ISBN 0-465-04994-X.

This study, supported by a grant from the National Institute on Aging, examines the role of grandparents in contemporary society. Today's grandparents are more likely to enjoy better education and many years of health and well-being. They also face new roles such as being stepgrandparents and, as divorce increases, they often play an active role in rearing some of their grandchildren. The grandparents interviewed in this study describe the tension alluded to in the book's title—how to maintain a satisfactory place in the family and at the same time keep their independence, or "a life apart." Although this is a scholarly work, it is clearly written, and the inclusion of real-life quotes makes it appealing to families as well as scholars.

Kingson, Eric R., et al. *Ties that Bind: The Interdependence of Generations.* Washington, DC: Seven Locks Press, 1986. 176p. $9.95, paper. ISBN 0-932020-44-5.

In the context of the debate over federal budgets and deficits, this book highlights issues and questions critical to the development of a framework for social policy. It analyzes existing and prospective arrangements for caregiving and examines the argument that the elderly are getting more than their share of health care monies. Clearly written for persons of all ages, it argues for interdependence in place of conflict among generations.

CHILDREN'S BOOKS

Aliki. *The Two of Them.* New York: Greenwillow, 1979. 32p. $12.95. ISBN 0-688-80225-7.

This little picture-book for preschool children presents a tender vignette of a small girl growing up as the apple of her grandfather's eye. When he becomes weak and sick, she cares for him as he did for her. When he dies, she knows her first real grief. This poignant story captures the essence of a true and lasting love between grandparent and grandchild.

Cooney, Barbara. *Miss Rumphius.* New York: Viking, 1982. Np. $13.95. ISBN 0-670-47958-6.

Great Aunt Alice Rumphius was once a little girl who loved the sea and wanted to travel to faraway places. Her grandfather told her she must also do something to make the world more beautiful. When she grew up she did all these things, and primary-age children will enjoy seeing just what she did to make the world more beautiful. This American Book Award winner presents a positive image of aging in a simple, beautiful story.

de Paola, Tomi A. *Now One Foot, Now the Other.* New York: G. P. Putnam's Sons, 1981. 48p. $9.95; $5.95, paper. ISBN 0-399-20774-0; 0-399-20775-9, paper.

This is the story of two best friends, Bobby and Grandfather Bob. When his grandfather suffers a stroke, Bobby teaches him to walk again, just as his grandfather had once taught Bobby. Children ages five to eight will enjoy this simple story of young Bobby learning and growing from this friendship.

Farber, Norma. *How Does It Feel To Be Old?* New York: E. P. Dutton, 1979. Np. $12.95. ISBN 0-525-32414-3.

This is a monologue in verse in which old age tells youth the advantages of being old. The author writes with honesty and wit about loneliness and love, about the past and the present, and about hope and memory linked in the relationship of a lonely old woman and a child. Suitable for grades four to six.

Fox, Mem. *Wilfred Gordon McDonald Partridge.* Brooklyn, NY: Kane/Miller, 1985. 32p. $12.95. ISBN 0-916-291-04-9.

Young Wilfred Gordon lives next door to a nursing home and is best friends with 96-year-old Miss Nancy. When Miss Nancy loses her memory, Wilfred decides to find it for her. He asks his elderly friends, "What's a memory?" and translates their abstract answers into things he can gather in a basket for Miss Nancy. Dreamy watercolors complement this warm, witty story. A beautiful, gentle story about aging that is suitable for children aged five to ten.

Guthrie, Donna. *Grandpa Doesn't Know It's Me.* New York: Human Sciences Press, 1986. Np. $14.95; $5.95, paper. ISBN 0-89885-302-8; 0-89885-308-7, paper.

This book is geared to the concerns of the young child who has a relative with Alzheimer's disease. It tells the story of Lizzie, who loves her grandpa very much and struggles with his loss of the memory of their past good times. It is a touching book, sensitively written. It helps open a dialog between the child and his or her family, making it easier for the child to come to terms with the situation.

Hest, Amy. *The Crack-of-Dawn Walkers.* New York: Macmillan, 1984. 32p. $11.95. ISBN 0-02-743710-8.

Sadie takes turns with her brother each Sunday morning walking with their grandfather, enjoying his attention and special treats. Grandfather is a European émigré with a sensitive, philosophical approach to the children. Young children will find this book a delight and appreciate Sadie's special times with her grandfather.

Horner, Catherine T. *The Aging Adult in Children's Books and Nonprint Media: An Annotated Bibliography.* Metuchen, NJ: Scarecrow Press, 1982. 265p. $22.50. ISBN 0-8108-1475-7.

This bibliography of juvenile literature lists fiction by age group, multimedia materials, resource materials, and textbooks and nonfiction books. There are author, title, and subject indexes to the multimedia section plus a directory of producers and distributors. The selections in this bibliography can be used by libraries, teachers, and parents to help sensitize children to elderly people.

MacLachlan, Patricia. *Through Grandpa's Eyes.* New York: Harper & Row, 1980. Np. $8.95. ISBN 0-06-02044-X.

John loves to be with his grandpa because he sees the world through Grandpa's eyes. Grandpa is blind, but he has his own way of seeing. He shows his grandson that the four other senses become sharper and can help a blind person enjoy nature and life to a degree that sighted persons can't. This warm, loving story of a young boy, his blind grandpa, and his wise grandma is good for ages six to nine.

Mathis, Sharon B. *The Hundred Penny Box.* New York: Viking, 1975. 47p. $13.95. ISBN 0-670-38787-8.

Conflict arises between Michael's mother and his father's Great Aunt Dewbet, who is 100, when they bring Great Aunt Dewbet to their small apartment. Chief among the problems is an old wooden box containing pennies, one for each birthday, that was started by Aunt Dew's late husband. Michael's mother wants to burn the old box and get a new one, while Michael tries to save the hundred penny box. Children in grades three to five will enjoy this remarkable story of the love between a very old woman and a young boy, who share their black roots in a very touching alliance.

Wittman, Sally. *A Special Trade.* New York: Harper & Row, 1978. Np. $10.89. ISBN 0-06-026554-X.

Nelly and Bartholomew are neighbors. When Nelly is small, Bartholomew pushes her in the stroller. They are always together as Nelly learns to walk and goes to school and learns to skate. As Bartholomew gets older, things start to change. But Nelly is older, too, and the change is really a trade—a special trade. Voted a Notable Children's Book by the American Library

Association, this is a whimsical story about friendship for very young children.

Zolotow, Charlotte. *I Know a Lady*. New York: Greenwillow, 1984. Np. $11.75. ISBN 0-688-03837-9.

Sally describes a loving and lovable old lady in her neighborhood who grows flowers, waves to children when they pass her house, and bakes goodies for them at Christmas and Easter. She is self-sufficient and friendly and inspires the child narrator to wonder about the old woman's childhood. Preschool and primary ages will like this lady who lives alone but has the neighborhood children for friends.

FILMS AND VIDEOCASSETTES

The Best of You, the Best of Me
Type: ¾" U-matic videocassette, ½" VHS or Beta videocassette, color
Length: 28 min.
Date: 1986
Cost: Purchase $100, rental $50
Source: Generations Together
University of Pittsburgh
811 William Pitt Union
Pittsburgh, PA 15260

This videotape demonstrates the importance of bringing young and old together for their mutual benefit. It is a sampler of intergenerational programs that portrays intergenerational exchanges in a variety of situations: a teenager helping a homebound frail elder, a group of high school students and older persons joining together in a unique drama experience, and elders sharing their love and skills with children in several settings. Included with the video is an instructional guide that makes the package suitable for educational systems, volunteer and civic groups, and human service agencies serving children, youth, and the elderly.

Close Harmony
Type: 16mm film, ½" VHS videocassette, black-and-white
Length: 30 min.
Date: 1981
Cost: Film $500; ½" VHS purchase $250, rental $75

Source: Learning Corporation of America
108 Wilmot Road
Deerfield, IL 60015-9990

Music teacher Arlene Symons teaches at an elementary school and leads group singing at senior centers. She decides to bring the two groups together in a concert. A pen-pal program helps the groups get acquainted and break down age-related barriers. The moment when the intergenerational chorus meets and performs together for the first time is magical, and the film captures it beautifully.

Long-Term Care

BOOKS

Estes, Carroll L., Charlene Harrington, and Robert J. Newcomer. *Long Term Care of the Elderly: Public Policy Issues.* Beverly Hills, CA: Sage, 1985. 280p. $35.00; $16.95, paper. ISBN 0-8039-2214-0; 0-8039-2215-9, paper.

The authors explore the tension between increasing needs and shrinking resources for long-term care, focus on state Medicaid policies and service delivery systems, present new data, and critique current policy shifts. The book is designed both as an introduction to the existing literature on long-term care issues and as an assessment of policy issues in order to provide a basic foundation of knowledge for advocates for the aging, professionals, and policymakers. Those who are planning or conducting research in long-term care will find the data useful.

Kane, Robert L., and Rosalie A. Kane. *A Will and a Way: What the United States Can Learn from Canada about Caring for the Elderly.* New York: Columbia University Press, 1985. 311p. $37.50. ISBN 0-231-06136-6.

This book is an analysis of the nursing home and home care systems in Canada. In that country, long-term care coverage is a universal benefit. The Kanes' report on long-term care as it is implemented in Ontario, Manitoba, and British Columbia and conclude that the cost-effective, quality care provided to the citizens of Canada is an example that the United States should heed. Health care planners and policymakers will find useful comparisons here.

Kane, Rosalie A., and Robert L. Kane. *Long-Term Care: Principles, Programs, and Policies.* New York: Springer, 1987. 422p. $34.95. ISBN 0-8261-6010-7.

Over the past few decades, long-term care has been a growth field. This comprehensive volume presents a thorough overview of existing long-term care systems including nursing home care, adult daycare, respite care, and programs for those living in their own homes. The authors describe the challenges of providing care to the frail elderly and review the evidence of the effectiveness of a wide variety of programs. Those responsible for policy in this field will find that this book presents the issues very clearly.

Karr, Katherine. *What Do I Do? How To Care for, Comfort and Commune with Your Nursing Home Elder.* New York: Haworth Press, 1985. 130p. $19.95, paper. ISBN 0-86656-398-9.

Family members may feel uncomfortable visiting their relatives in nursing homes. It's not easy to know what to do or talk about. This book will help families feel connected to and actively involved with their nursing home relatives. It addresses the physical, mental, emotional, and spiritual needs of the older person by identifying concerns for each area. Also included are specific suggestions for increasing or strengthening family participation, tips on improving communication, and steps families can take to bring problems to staff's attention.

Mendleson, Mary A. *Tender Loving Greed: How the Incredibly Lucrative Nursing Home Industry Is Exploiting America's Old People and Defrauding Us All.* New York: Knopf, 1974. 245p. OP. ISBN 0-394-47597-6.

This well-documented indictment of nursing home abuses should be read by anyone who believes that "nursing homes are doing the very best they can." This reporting of these abuses, of government failure to enforce laws, and of public apathy surrounding nursing homes sparked government action.

Rabin, David L., and Patricia Stockton. *Long-Term Care for the Elderly: A Factbook.* New York: Oxford University Press, 1987. 248p. $35.00; $14.95, paper. ISBN 0-19-504102-X; 0-19-504106-2, paper.

This book is designed as a concise reference source of national data relevant to long-term care. Topic areas include population growth and change, mortality, morbidity, health care expenditures and utilization, and growth and change in the nursing home sector. There is information on legislation, regulation, and recent policy issues. All those who have a professional interest in the problems of caring for the elderly or who are involved with program planning will value this guide.

Richards, Marty, et al. *Choosing a Nursing Home: A Guidebook for Families.* Seattle: University of Washington Press, 1985. 110p. $8.95. ISBN 0-295-96221-6.

The goal of this publication is to assist families or friends with making a decision about placing an older adult in a nursing home. The early chapters help by discussing feelings around the decision; once the decision is reached, the guide can assist in choosing a nursing home, understanding legal and financial intricacies, adjusting to the changes, and helping the friend or relative. With its extremely practical suggestions, this book will help relatives and friends feel less confused by the burden of providing care.

Rothert, Eugene A., and James R. Daubert. *Horticultural Therapy for Nursing Homes, Senior Centers, Retirement Living.* Glencoe, IL: Chicago Horticultural Society, 1981. 130p. $10. ISBN 0-939914-01-8.

Almost everyone has grown something at one time or another. Using horticulture as therapy is becoming more popular, and this manual specializes in horticultural therapy for the elderly. There are indoor and outdoor gardening programs plus suggestions for nature crafts, information on obtaining community support for the program, and lists of resource materials. The information supplied here is valuable to the retired person living alone or in a retirement community as well as to those working within the field of aging. There is particular emphasis on adapting the programs for nursing home residents who have a high degree of physical limitation and lack of motivation.

Sandel, Susan L., and David R. Johnson. *Waiting at the Gate: Creativity and Hope in the Nursing Home.* New York: Haworth Press, 1987. 120p. $24.95. ISBN 0-86656-631-7.

The authors, who are dance and drama therapists, have compiled some of their previously published articles to create a book presenting both theoretical discussion and case examples of the effect of movement and drama therapies on nursing home residents. They offer discussion of their failures as well as their successes, which makes the book a valuable teaching tool. The articles are clearly written and will be understandable even to those unfamiliar with dance and drama therapies.

Tisdale, Sallie. *Harvest Moon: Portrait of a Nursing Home.* New York: Henry Holt and Company, 1987. 204p. $17.95. ISBN 0-8050-0565-X.

Harvest Moon helps remove some of the mystery that surrounds nursing home living. Tisdale, a registered nurse, immersed herself in the daily routines at a 100-bed facility, and the result is a detailed inside look into the personal and practical issues of nursing home living. There are many readable vignettes about nursing home life as told by patients and staff. Tisdale also describes all aspects of running a nursing home, from cooking the meals to the low pay and status of nurse's aides. For families who are unfamiliar with the details of nursing home living, *Harvest Moon* provides a realistic and complete picture of the activities, people, and regulations that make up life in a long-term care facility.

William, J. Winston, ed. *Marketing Long-Term and Senior Care Services.* New York: Haworth Press, 1984. 113p. $29.95. ISBN 0-86656-289-3. (Also published as *Health Marketing Quarterly* Vol. 1, No. 4, Summer 1984.)

The various articles in this volume elaborate on why marketing is needed for senior care services, provide examples of specific marketing strategies, describe how services for seniors differ from other health services, and discuss factors in consumer selection of senior services. While recognizing that in nonprofit circles the term *marketing* has certain negative connotations, the authors agree that it is a necessary component of managing a nursing home, a residential care facility, or a day health care program. Those who are trying to attract clients to their long-term care service will find this book helpful.

PERIODICALS

Contemporary Long-Term Care. 12/yr. $27. P.O. Box 8391-44320, Akron, OH 44320.

This magazine covers both nursing homes and retirement centers, and though it is not limited to health care issues, that is the greatest emphasis. Articles range from sample menus to redecorating to computerizing records to heading off employee attempts to unionize. There is a special pull-out section for directors of nursing with information on patient care.

There is an annual *Product Directory and Buyers Guide* as well as special supplements on new products.

Nursing Homes and Senior Citizen Care. 6/yr. $28. Nursing Homes, 5615 West Cermak Road, Cicero, IL 60650.

This magazine is designed to be of interest to administrators of nursing homes and other long-term care facilities. It considers issues on the use of restraints, architecture, options for financing long-term care, and staff development. There is a also a pull-out section, "Family Matters," that contains information for family members of nursing home residents, which administrators can duplicate for their residents' families. New products are featured as well as briefs on legal matters and government policies.

AUDIOVISUAL RESOURCES

And the Home of the Brave
Type: ½" VHS and Beta videocassette, color
Length: 17 min.
Date: 1989
Cost: Purchase $275, rental $50
Source: Tricepts Productions
          Film Library
          445 West Main Street
          Wyckoff, NJ 07481

In *And the Home of the Brave,* Lillian Ross finds her name has become "honey" upon entering a nursing home. Her new roommate, Bertha, is patronized by a nurse when her dream of moving into her son's home is shattered by his divorce. Offered with a study guide, this short videotape is designed to sensitize nursing home staff and gerontology students to the viewpoints and feelings of residents. It touches many sensitive bases in 17 minutes and will generate passionate discussions in spite of its brevity.

Best Wishes, Edith and Henry!
Type: Slides/audiotape
Length: 18 min.
Date: 1984
Cost: Purchase $40, rental $10

Source: Dr. Vicki Schmall
           161 Milam Hall
           Oregon State University
           Corvalis, OR 97331

This program features Edith (75) and Henry (81) and their adult children, who are worried about their parents' failing health and ability to remain independent. At a family conference all concerns are shared, and everyone is relieved they have had this open talk. The viewer next sees Henry in need of nursing home care and is made aware of the importance of planning ahead and of open, honest family communication. This program is basically cheerful but also realistic, with guidelines for decision making and preventive action. This is an excellent presentation for community groups and for introducing families to the issues involved in assisting aging parents.

Peege
Type: 16mm film, ½" VHS videocassette, color
Length: 28 min.
Date: 1974
Cost: Film purchase $560, rental $40; ½" VHS $325
Source: BFA Education Media
           A Division of Phoenix Films
           468 Park Avenue, South
           New York, NY 10016

This film depicts a Christmas visit to a blind, stroke-crippled grandmother in a nursing home. The family's difficult visit to the institution is sensitively handled, and the oldest grandson is able to break through the silence imposed by failing faculties to reach his grandmother and affirm his love. This is a touching drama of love and a testament to the special part grandparents play in our lives.

Seven Days a Week
Type: 16mm film, ½" VHS and Beta videocassette, color
Length: 30 min.
Date: 1987
Cost: Film purchase $495, rental $50; ½" VHS and Beta purchase $375, rental $50
Source: Terra Nova Films, Inc.
           9848 South Winchester Avenue
           Chicago, IL 60643

This documentary, made over a period of nine months, shows the many facets of living and working in a nursing home. The administrator fosters a holistic view of the patient and scenes of the everyday operation of the nursing home show staff training, activity programs, and numerous interactions between residents, staff, and family. *Seven Days a Week* shows how staff training, teamwork that includes the patient, mutual responsibility, and administrative support contribute to quality nursing home care. This film is especially good for medical, nursing, occupational therapy and physical therapy students, nursing home administrators, and staff.

Wesley Hall: A Special Life
Type: 16mm film, ½" VHS and Beta videocassette, color
Length: 28 min.
Date: 1986
Cost: Film purchase $365, rental $50; ½" VHS and Beta purchase $245, rental $50
Source: Terra Nova Films, Inc.
          9848 South Winchester Avenue
          Chicago, IL 60643

This 28-minute overview identifies the philosophy behind Wesley Hall, a pilot project aimed at creating an environment in which institutionalized victims of Alzheimer's disease thrive, living with dignity and minimizing functional loss. Staff received special training to provide a warm, supportive environment in which residents have the opportunity to maintain social roles. Family members, staff, and administrators discuss how the project has enabled the residents to experience a life of joy, love, and dignity. The facility's design and operation issues are also discussed. This is an excellent training tool for professional staff and facility planners.

Mental Health

BOOKS

Billig, Nathan. *To Be Old and Sad: Understanding Depression in the Elderly.* Lexington, MA: Lexington Books, 1987. 128p. $21.95; $8.95, paper. ISBN 0-669-12277-7; 0-669-12279-3, paper.

Billig, a leading authority on geriatric psychiatry, shows that depression in the elderly is not inevitable, that it is a very painful condition for older people and their families, and that safe and effective treatments are available. The author describes the biological and social changes that may predispose an older person to depression. Using case studies, he describes the signs and symptoms of depression, the important differences between dementia and depression in an older person, the various treatments available, and the importance of involving family members in treatment. Written in straightforward language and filled with basic information, this book is useful for families with elderly members, for older adults who are concerned about the possibility of depression, and for students in fields concerned with aging.

Birren, James E., and K. Warner Schaie, eds. *Handbook of the Psychology of Aging.* 3rd ed. New York: Harcourt Brace, 1989. 501p. $65. ISBN 0-12-101280-8.

This classic handbook provides students with up-to-date research in established as well as new areas of the psychology of aging. New scientific areas covered range from behavioral genetics and the ecology of aging to arousal, sleep, and the vestibular function. The handbook is a basic source for studies both in psychology and gerontology.

Birren, James E., and R. Bruce Sloane, eds. *Handbook of Mental Health and Aging.* Englewood Cliffs, NJ: Prentice-Hall, 1980. 1064p. $114. ISBN 0-13-380261-2.

Handbook of Mental Health and Aging is a definitive reference book in which specialists discuss comprehensive treatments of adult behaviors and the ways in which biological and environmental influences affect the aging process. Major areas covered include current social issues, genetics, learning, memory, personality adjustment, environment, depression, sexuality, relaxation, and exercise. This book will assist professionals engaged in providing services for older adults.

Burnside, Irene M. *Working with the Elderly: Group Process and Techniques.* 2nd ed. Boston, MA: Jones & Bartlett Publishers, 1986. Reprint of 1984 ed. $30. ISBN 0-86720-379-X.

Still the only text of its kind that deals exclusively with group work and the elderly, this second edition has been expanded to include 19 new chapters written by contributors from even more disciplines. These new chapters include self-help groups, reminiscing, therapy, and perspectives from the disciplines of nursing, social work, music therapy, and volunteerism. There is a brief history of group work with the elderly in the United States. The book then focuses on the general knowledge needed to start and maintain groups and the practical aspects of leading groups of all types. The practice exercises, bibliographies, and lists of resources accompanying each chapter make this a valuable text for practitioners and students specializing in geriatric care.

Butler, Robert N., and Myrna L. Lewis. *Aging and Mental Health.* 3rd ed. Columbus, OH: Merrill Publishing Co., 1982. 483p. $29.95, paper. ISBN 0-675-20610-3.

Stating that ageism contributes significantly to the generally negative opinion about mental health care for older adults, the authors set out to dispel some of the traditional diagnostic and treatment myths. They focus on treating the individual from birth to death in a coherent manner and, to that end, include—as mental health specialists—nurses, nurse's aides, technicians, the clergy, and homemakers, all of whom typically work with the elderly. In their first two editions they emphasized positive psychosocial approaches in mental health care of older people. This third edition includes biomedical approaches by presenting new biomedical findings that are currently being incorporated into treatment. All who deal with the emotional crises confronting older people will benefit from reading this book.

Eisdorfer, Carl, and Donna Cohen. *Mental Health Care of the Aging: A Multidisciplinary Curriculum for Professional Training.* New York: Springer, 1982. 131p. $23.95. ISBN 0-8261-4090-4.

The authors identify important areas of knowledge for the training of mental health professionals in the field of aging and provide a long, detailed outline that can be used in preparing a curriculum. Subjects include biomedical aspects of aging, social and community services, and policy issues. The book covers such topics as clinical manifestations of psychopathology, diagnosis, and treatment modalities. This is an advanced training program that can be adapted to pre-professional training goals as well. This model curriculum will help faculty organize a program in mental health care of the aged and will facilitate research and teaching.

Herr, John J., and John H. Weakland. *Counseling Elders and Their Families: Practical Techniques for Applied Gerontology.* Vol. 2 of Springer Series on Adulthood and Aging. New York: Springer, 1979. 308p. $21.95; OP, paper. ISBN 0-8261-2510-7; 0-8261-2511-5, paper.

Herr and Weakland present a format for approaching the problems of the older adult in the family context. While addressing the problems of physical and mental health, income, and loneliness, the authors help us understand how families can be more effective in meeting the needs of their older family members. This book is useful for social workers, family counselors, administrators, physicians, nurses, psychiatrists, and families of older adults. The authors stress the need for compassionate understanding and the importance of letting clients reach their own decisions rather than selecting solutions for them.

Hinrichsen, Gregory A. *Mental Health Problems and Older Adults.* Santa Barbara, CA: ABC-CLIO, 1990. 300p. $39.50. ISBN 0-87436-240-7. (In Choices and Challenges: An Older Adult Reference Series.)

This book discusses major issues in the nature, frequency, diagnosis, treatment, and prognosis of the most common mental health problems that affect older adults. It provides a general orientation to cognitive problems, problems such as schizophrenia and delusional disorders, substance use disorders, and practical suggestions for finding and using mental health services. There is a resource section of organizations—local, state, and national—concerned with mental health and aging, an annotated bibliography of books, and reviews of films and videocassettes on mental health and aging. Currently, there is very little information available for the general public on the diagnosis and treatment of late life mental disorders. This book will fill that need for professionals, older people, and their families who want to become familiar with recent developments in the mental health field.

Kemper, Donald W., et al., eds. *Growing Wiser: The Older Person's Guide to Mental Wellness.* Boise, ID: Healthwise, Inc., 1986. 122p. $10. ISBN 0-9612690-3-0.

Presented in a workbook format, *Growing Wiser* will help older people expand and exercise their mental vitality. Through exercises and activities, the reader is aided in improving memory and mental alertness, gaining insight into loss and life changes, becoming more assertive, and maintaining a positive environment. This is a practical, helpful guide to dealing with the challenges of aging.

Miller, Mary. *Suicide after Sixty: The Final Alternative.* Vol. 2 of Springer Series on Death and Suicide. New York: Springer, 1979. 118p. OP; OP, paper. ISBN 0-8261-2780-0; 0-8261-2781-9, paper.

Miller documents and analyzes the multiple losses in old age that have serious effects on the elderly—effects so devastating that each year the proportion of suicides among older persons outweighs that of any other age group. Fixed incomes, declining health, dependency, loss of a spouse, and institutionalization can create unbearable conditions, and Miller uses case histories to discuss different reactions to these losses. The book also looks at the relation between geriatric suicide and euthanasia and has an extensive appendix that contains a critique of the research on geriatric suicides, along with conclusions to date and suggestions for future research. This is a book for students, professionals, and family members.

Osgood, Nancy J. *Suicide in the Elderly: A Practitioner's Guide to Diagnosis and Mental Health Intervention.* Rockville, MD: Aspen Systems Corp., 1985. 240p. $49. ISBN 0-87189-088-7.

This book is written for all those working with the elderly who want to know why older adults are likely to commit suicide and how to recognize and help such individuals. The emphasis is on identifying potential suicide victims in the elderly population and on specifying appropriate assessment techniques and interventions that can be employed by professionals working with the elderly. There are profiles of the at-risk elderly; assessment scales and techniques to measure depression, life satisfaction, loneliness, and stress; and specific counseling techniques and strategies.

Robinson, Anne, Beth Spencer, and Laurie White, eds. *Understanding Difficult Behaviors: Some Practical Suggestions for Coping with Alzheimer's Disease and Related Illnesses.* Ypsilanti, MI: Geriatric Education Center of Michigan, 1989. Various paging. $10. No ISBN. Order from: Turner Geriatric Services Publications, 1010 Wall Street, Ann Arbor, MI 48109-0714.

Written for caregivers in both home and long-term care settings, this book focuses on common problem areas, teaching the reader to identify causes and to make a plan of action to cope with the situation. The authors emphasize the importance of good communication between caregiver and patient while describing techniques for improving verbal and nonverbal communication, to help caregivers cope with difficult behaviors and to ease the stress experienced by patients. This book is an excellent resource for caregivers of dementia patients.

Safford, Florence. *Caring for the Mentally Impaired Elderly: A Family Guide.* New York: Henry Holt and Company, 1989. 336p. $12.95, paper. ISBN 0-8050-1041-6.

Here is critically important advice on how to recognize the signs and symptoms of mental impairment and how to distinguish mental impairment from the normal aging process. Written by a medical social worker for families helping disoriented elderly, this book offers information on how to deal with doctors; how to make use of community services; how to obtain home care; and, should it become necessary, how to choose institutional care and get financial assistance and when to assume legal and financial guardianships. This is an excellent guide to understanding the nature of the problems that face the family caring for a mentally impaired elder.

Teri, Linda, and Peter M. Lewinsohn, eds. *Geropsychological Assessment and Treatment: Selected Topics.* New York: Springer, 1986. 224p. $25.95. ISBN 0-8261-4790-9.

This book is not a comprehensive textbook on how to assess and treat all problems faced by older adults. As the title suggests, the editors have limited the subject matter to specific assessment and treatment strategies for chronic pain and behavioral and sexual problems. This book will provide the mental health practitioner and practitioner-in-training with a practical but scholarly guide to assessment and treatment of some of the primary psychological problems facing older adults.

PERIODICAL

Clinical Gerontologist: The Journal of Aging and Mental Health. 4/yr. $32, individuals. $82, institutions. $125, libraries. Haworth Press, 10 Alice Street, Binghamton, NY 13904.

This journal is oriented toward the psychological and psychiatric issues in care of the elderly. Articles include research reports, reviews of the literature, and case material on topics of interest to the practitioner—paranoia in late life, poetry group therapy, and treatment of geriatric alcoholics, for example. There are also book, audiovisual media, and software reviews.

Minorities

BOOKS

Applewhite, Steven R., ed. *Hispanic Elderly in Transition.* Westport, CT: Greenwood Press, 1988. 252p. $39.95. ISBN 0-313-24478-2.

This volume of essays attempts to synthesize health, economic, social, and cultural issues influencing the quality of life for elderly Hispanics. Demographic trends point to a growth of the Hispanic population, but Hispanic elderly remain underserved in terms of social services. Non-Hispanic practitioners can learn from this one volume the fundamental issues facing the Hispanic elderly, and researchers will find here a starting point for studies of this group.

Becerra, Rosina M. *The Hispanic Elderly: A Research Reference Guide.* Lanham, MD: University Press of America, 1984. 152p. $29.75; $13.00, paper. ISBN 0-8191-3626-3; 0-8191-3627-1, paper.

This is a comprehensive review of the literature to identify research on the Hispanic elderly. The review lists research in which the Hispanic elderly have been the central focus of investigation or in which they are a subsample of larger investigations. For researchers interested in the Hispanic population, this guide provides a source of Spanish-language research instruments as well as information and statistics on the special needs, experiences, and concerns of elderly Hispanics.

Gelfand, Donald E. *Aging, the Ethnic Factor.* Boston, MA: Little, Brown, 1982. 113p. OP; OP, paper. ISBN 0-316-30713-0; 0-316-30714-9, paper.

In this examination of ethnic aged persons, with an emphasis on their sociocultural characteristics, the author focuses on the question of resources and needs of the ethnic elderly. He studies the role of ethnicity in support systems for the elderly and in health, mental health, and social services for aged citizens and provides a direction for future efforts in the area of ethnicity and aging. Researchers and service providers will find that this volume will help provide data needed to include ethnicity as a major variable in any sociological or psychological research or planning effort for aged citizens.

Gelfand, Donald E., and Charles M. Barresi, eds. *Ethnic Dimensions of Aging.* New York: Springer, 1987. 299p. $31.95. ISBN 0-8261-5610-X.

The contributors to this work present a broad spectrum on the topic. Specific cultures included are Hmong, Amish, Japanese, Canadian, Greek, black, and Mexican elderly, among others. The authors stress the need to go beyond simple identification of ethnic groups and look at interactions by class, sex, generation, etc. Various research methodologies are described and both clinical and policy issues are addressed. The material presented should be useful for both students and practitioners in this area.

Jones, Reginald L., ed. *Black Adult Development and Aging.* Berkeley, CA: Cobb & Henry, 1989. 429p. $36.95; $25.95, paper. ISBN 0-943539-03-X; 0-943539-04-8, paper.

This is a book about the development and aging of black American adults across the entire lifespan from early adulthood to old age. The perspective is multidisciplinary with contributors representing several disciplines including psychology, sociology, economics, social work, and the biological sciences. Researchers and students looking for studies on black early and middle adulthood, both rare subjects of investigation, will be pleased to find the information contained here as well as the chapters specifically on the black elderly.

Kehoe, Monika. *Lesbians over 60 Speak for Themselves.* New York: Haworth Press, 1989. 111p. $19.95. ISBN 0-86656-816-6. (Also published as the *Journal of Homosexuality* Vol. 16, Nos. 3/4, 1988.)

There are an estimated 1 million-plus lesbians over 60 in the United States, and Kehoe's study of 100 older lesbians provides a look at this little-known group. The women interviewed do not, as do most older women, stress health and economic issues as their primary problems. Rather, their concerns all relate to social issues, deriving from the double prejudice against aging and homosexuality. There are very few networks for older homosexuals, and the women in Kehoe's study express a sense of isolation and vulnerability; all express the wish that there were lesbian retirement communities. Kehoe's groundbreaking study provides a new insight into aging in the United States.

Marguia, Edward, et al. *Ethnicity and Aging: A Bibliography.* San Antonio, TX: Trinity University Press, 1984. 132p. $18. ISBN 0-939980-03-7.

Combining ethnic studies and gerontology, this bibliography reflects the growth in the last 20 years of both these areas of academic inquiry. The work deals only with U.S. elderly ethnic and racial groups. It is divided into ethnic and racial categories and then into topical subcategories (e.g., "Native Americans: Death and Dying"). Within each subject grouping, items are arranged alphabetically by author's name. This comprehensive, multi-ethnic bibliography on aging will assist researchers, teachers, and policymakers.

Vacha, Keith. *Quiet Fire: Memoirs of Older Gay Men.* Trumansburg, NY: Crossing Press, 1985. 219p. $22.95. ISBN 0-89594-158-9.

Vacha presents feelings and thoughts in the words of gays themselves, beginning with their earliest childhood memories to their current status as older persons. Interviews of 100 gays and lesbians 55 years or older covered a period of six years, from 1978 to 1984. These life histories sketch similarities between heterosexual and homosexual lives in seeking caring relationships, in compromises and communications essential to maintain those relationships, in the struggle to integrate or separate the requirements of work and personal life, in adjustments to ageism, and in life after the death of a longtime partner. This collection of personal portraits is a welcome addition to the generally statistical, analytical articles and studies of gay life.

PERIODICAL

The Journal of Minority Aging. 2/yr. $30. National Council on Black Aging, P.O. Box 8813, Durham, NC 27707.

This is a scholarly journal on research and policy issues pertaining to aging or the conditions of aging among minorities, including women. The major emphasis is on black aging, but other minorities and their problems are covered. The scope is not restricted to the United States. The articles consider research from a sociological viewpoint and comparative studies are included.

FILM AND VIDEOCASSETTE

Number Our Days
Type: 16mm film, ½" VHS videocassette, black-and-white
Length: 29 min.
Date: 1978

Cost: Film purchase $495, rental $55; ½" VHS purchase $250, rental $55
Source: Direct Cinema, Ltd.
        Mitchell Block
        P.O. Box 69589
        Los Angeles, CA 90069

This film is based on a book of the same name authored by the late anthropologist Barbara Myerhoff. She documented a community of elderly Eastern European Jews who make the Israel Levin Senior Adult Center in Venice, California, the center of their lives. This unique film shows how these elderly Jews maintain their cultural heritage while contending with loneliness and poverty.

Public Policy

BOOKS

Bass, Scott, et al., eds. *Diversity in Aging: Challenges Facing Planners and Policymakers in the 1990s.* Des Plaines, IL: Scott, Foresman, 1989. 208p. OP. ISBN 0-673-24933-6.

Topics covered in this futuristic volume include demographic projections, the need for culturally sensitive practices when providing services to elders, ways to respond to the most vulnerable elderly, challenges in responding to diversity within U.S. political and economic constraints, the politics of productivity versus the politics of entitlement, and a vision of elderly leadership for a diverse nation. This book will spark discussion among human services professionals, advocates for the elderly, legislators, and public policymakers.

Estes, Carroll. *The Aging Enterprise.* San Francisco, CA: Jossey-Bass, 1979. 283p. $27.95. ISBN 0-87589-410-0.

In this controversial examination of the Older Americans Act and 80 federal programs for the elderly, Estes says that "social policies for the aged in the United States are a failure. This failure is socially constructed and is based on our attitudes toward the aged, as well as our political, economic, and social structures." In this book she suggests a more universal approach as well as specific changes that would more effectively meet the needs of the aged.

Gilford, Dorothy M., ed. *The Aging Population in the Twenty-First Century: Statistics for Health Policy.* Washington, DC: National Academy Press, 1988. 323p. $19.95. ISBN 0-309-03881-2.

This study by the National Research Council addresses the inadequacies of statistical information and methodology available for future policy decisions concerning the elderly. The book discusses the social, economic, and demographic trends that trigger policy issues and the data requirements for policy development and recommends actions needed to ensure that these data will be available. These recommendations will be of interest to health professionals engaged in long-range planning for the elderly population.

Lammers, William W. *Public Policy and the Aging.* Washington, DC: CQ Press, 1983. 265p. $9.50. ISBN 0-87187-246-3.

Among the political and public policy questions explored in this text are: What changes can be expected in labor force participation by persons over 65? What are the battles over Social Security about? Are aging-based interest groups effective on Capitol Hill? Do elderly women face different problems from elderly men? In examining these issues the author explains why the rapid expansion of the aged population has occurred and how it will affect the development of programs for the elderly in the United States. This book will clarify policies on aging for academic and professional audiences.

Leutz, Walter N., et al. *Changing Health Care for An Aging Society: Planning for the Social Health Maintenance Organization.* Lexington, MA: Lexington Books, 1985. 252p. OP. ISBN 0-669-10139-7.

The social health maintenance organization (SHMO) is an integrated approach to acute and long-term care for the elderly. It combines current expenditures by Medicare, Medicaid, and individuals as revenue sources, and it uses this pooled financing to pay for both acute and chronic care. The concept originated at Brandeis's Heller Graduate School and led to four demonstration projects whose programs form the basis for this book. The authors analyze the issues and obstacles that were addressed in operating the programs and document the programs' achievements. The SHMO is a concept about which very little has been written, so this book will be an invaluable resource for policymakers and future SHMO sponsors.

Neugarten, Bernice L., ed. *Age or Need? Public Policies for Older People.* Beverly Hills, CA: Sage, 1982. 288p. $35; $14, paper. ISBN 0-8039-1908-5; 0-8039-1909-3, paper.

This significant and controversial book addresses the question whether age per se is the best criterion for designing and implementing major public programs for older people. Questions posed include: Do age-based benefits reinforce negative stereotypes about older people? Would a new emphasis on need, rather than age, undo recent improvements in the general well-being of older people? Of use to social scientists, policymakers, and students, this book first helped inform the public debate on the issue and is still frequently cited in the examination of present policies and programs.

Rivlin, Alice M., and Joshua M. Wiener. *Caring for the Disabled Elderly: Who Will Pay?* Washington, DC: Brookings Institution, 1988. 318p. $31.95; $11.95, paper. ISBN 0-8157-7498-2; 0-8157-7497-4, paper.

Providing long-term care for the elderly has become one of the major social problems in the United States. As the baby boom generation ages and people live longer, the demand for long-term care will rise sharply. This study analyzes the major options for reforming the ways long-term care is financed—private long-term care insurance, individual medical accounts, home equity conversions, continuing care retirement communities, public long-term care insurance, modifications of Medicare and Medicaid, and block grants. The study recommends both a greatly expanded role for the private sector in financing long-term care and a new public insurance program. This research will be useful to those who are developing public policy around organization and financing of long-term care.

PERIODICAL

Older Americans Report (OAR). Weekly. $252. Business Publishers, Inc., 951 Pershing Drive, Silver Spring, MD 20910-4464.

This weekly ten-page newsletter is the best resource for keeping up-to-date on current federal legislation affecting the elderly. Along with reports on bills and budgets, *OAR* publishes personnel changes on key committees on aging, follows congressional committee activities, reports pertinent state and local news, and announces the availability of funding through federal grants. Specialists working with the aged, researchers in the field, and policy planners will value the currency of *OAR*'s information.

Recreation and Leisure

BOOKS

Chambré, Susan M. *Good Deeds in Old Age: Volunteering by the New Leisure Class.* Lexington, MA: Lexington Books, 1987. 224p. $25. ISBN 0-669-13091-5.

Based on the first major study of elderly volunteers, this book analyzes the kinds of satisfaction gained from volunteering and charts the influences leading to the decision to volunteer. From her conclusions, the author offers suggestions for programs designed to foster elderly volunteers and recommends ways to make volunteering more attractive to elderly people.

Coberly, Lenore M., et al. *Writers Have No Age: Creative Writing with Older Adults.* Binghamton, NY: Haworth Press, 1985. 128p. $24.95. ISBN 0-86656-320-2.

This book is a guide for the teaching of creative writing to older adults. It identifies likely students and suitable teachers and outlines appropriate procedures for starting and continuing writing classes. In addition to providing a framework and rationale for programming, the book features a set of detailed lesson plans and provides listings of lesson and teacher resources.

Harris, Robert W. *Gypsying after 40: A Guide to Adventure & Self-Discovery.* Santa Fe, NM: John Muir Publications, 1987. 253p. $12.95. ISBN 0-912528-71-0.

Whether they do it by boat, van, or car, this book will encourage and guide those who have a vision of taking time off to travel for an extended period. The author gives practical tips on money, health, camping, safety, food, and bargain destinations. He instills in readers a sense of adventure and the pleasures of the gypsy life and then explains how to make these dreams a reality.

Lerman, Liz. *Teaching Dance to Senior Adults.* Springfield, IL: Charles Thomas, 1984. 167p. $23.75. ISBN 0-398-04903-3.

The author describes a successful technique used in working with the elderly to create dances both for their own satisfaction and for public performances. The social and therapeutic aspects of the program are demonstrated and there is helpful information on the administration and financing of the program as well. Many of the people who would most benefit from the information in this book are not dancers. Recreational therapists, activity directors, and administrators of facilities for the elderly would find this program helpful to their clients.

Massow, Rosaline. *Travel Easy: The Practical Guide for People over 50.* Washington, DC: American Association of Retired Persons and Scott, Foresman, 1987. 286p. $8.95. ISBN 0-673-24817-8.

Packed with tips on everything from choosing a destination to dealing with lost luggage, this travel book eases the anxieties of both new and seasoned travelers. Included are advice on traveling alone, pros and cons of organized tours, discounts for older citizens, and customs such as tipping in foreign countries. Age is no barrier to rewarding travel adventures, but lack of information can be. The fact that this travel book has pertinent suggestions for the older traveler sets it apart from other guides.

Olsen, Nancy. *Starting a Mini-Business: A Guidebook for Seniors and Others Who Dream of Having Their Own Part-Time, Home-Based Business.* Sunnyvale, CA: Fairoaks Publishing Co., 1988. Rev. ed. 144p. $8.95. ISBN 0-933271-02-6.

Starting a Mini-Business is a complete, practical guide to beginning a very small-scale business. There are tips on finding a good idea, suggestions for affordable advertising, examples of simple record-keeping, and advice on basic legal requirements. The book contains resource lists and helpful exercises for use in creating a business plan. This guidebook is easy to understand and encouraging to seniors who want to begin a very small-scale business.

Selden, Ira Lee. *Going into Business for Yourself: New Beginnings after 50.* Washington, DC: American Association of Retired Persons and Scott, Foresman, 1988. 245p. $8.95. ISBN 0-673-24882-8.

Going into Business is clear, specific, easy to read, and inexpensive. Of special interest to retirees are the chapters on "new beginnings" and the impact, especially of taxes, on a person's financial position. Other chapters offer advice on topics from creating a legal structure and obtaining financing to working at home. In fact, anyone contemplating plunging into their own business would profit from Selden's realistic advice.

Weisberg, Naida, and Rosilyn Wilder, eds. *Creative Arts with Older Adults.* New York: Human Sciences Press, 1985. 252p. $34.95; $16.95, paper. ISBN 0-89885-161-0; 0-89885-163-7, paper.

This sourcebook presents specific experiences and theories by outstanding creative arts leaders and therapists working with older adults in nursing homes, community centers, and psychiatric institutions. All illustrate how the techniques of drama, music, art, dance, poetry, and prose can contribute to the vitality and social interaction of both alert and confused as well as ambulatory and nonambulatory older people. This program-oriented book will be of help to art therapy practitioners and to those trying to fund creative arts services for older adults.

PERIODICAL

Heartland Journal. 3/yr. $12. P.O. Box 55115, Madison, WI 53705.

This large-print journal contains prose, poetry, history, and personal experiences written by older adults. Themes have included love, relationships, relatives, reminiscences, and special issues of photographic works created by men and women over 60. The work is high quality and very engaging and will appeal to readers of all ages.

FILM AND VIDEOCASSETTE

Ruth Stout's Garden
Type: 16mm film, ½" VHS videocassette, color
Length: 23 min.
Date: 1976
Cost: Film purchase $450, rental $45; ½" VHS purchase $390, rental $45
Source: Arthur Makin
              P.O. Box 1866
              Santa Rosa, CA 95402-1866

This film consists of a visit with Ruth Stout as she talks about and works in her "no dig, no work" garden. She describes the methods she uses, which are both ecologically sound and productive. Stout's commentary as she describes her attitudes toward life, her family, and her interests make this an enjoyable film about creative aging that is suitable for all ages.

Resources and Human Services

BOOKS

Averyt, Anne C. *Successful Aging: A Sourcebook for Older People and Their Families.* New York: Ballantine Books, 1987. 526p. $9.95. ISBN 0-345-33331-4.

This sourcebook is designed to let older people and their families know what resources exist, where they are, what they provide, and how to contact them. It is divided into chapters that discuss retirement and financial planning, women alone, housing, health, nutrition, death and bereavement, and other areas of concern to older people. This book has an easy-to-follow format that will make informed consumers out of its readers.

Developing Adult Day Care: An Approach to Maintaining Independence for Impaired Older Persons. Washington, DC: National Council on the Aging, 1982. Np. $15. No ISBN.

Adult daycare is one of many services intended to help the families of impaired adults as well as other caregivers keep giving a little longer. The term *adult daycare* is used to describe a variety of arrangements that provide care in a supervised group setting away from home. *Developing Adult Day Care* discusses the place of adult daycare in the long-term care service continuum, essential and optional services, and program examples. It will provide guidance for community planners, administrators, adult daycare staff, and volunteers as they consider and develop daycare programs.

Gelfand, Donald E. *The Aging Network: Programs and Services.* 3rd ed. New York: Springer, 1988. 320p. $19.95. ISBN 0-8261-3054-2.

Revised and updated, this essential text describes the key components in a multitude of programs serving the aged on federal, state, and local levels. The book explores programs in health, transportation, crime recovery and legal assistance, employment and volunteer opportunities, and nutrition for the elderly and provides an understanding of basic program premises. There is an effort to clarify the goals, target populations, and important components of specific programs and services so that practitioners planning future programs will be better equipped. Students of gerontology, practitioners at all levels, and older persons themselves will find this book to be a valuable and practical guide to the full range of services for older persons.

Huttman, Elizabeth D. *Social Services for the Elderly.* New York: Free Press, 1985. 296p. $24.95. ISBN 02-915600-9.

Believing strongly in the continuum of care concept, the author lays out a full range of services that can help the older person who is trying to maintain a maximal level of independent functioning. These include linkage and protective services, special contact services, meals services and transportation programs, housing programs, adult daycare, long-term care services, and the informal support system of family and community. Huttman defines various services, cites program examples and funding sources, and discusses problems associated with provision of each service. This is a useful resource to anyone who wants to understand the assortment of social services available to the elderly.

Le Fevre, Carol, and Perry Le Fevre, eds. *Aging and the Human Spirit: A Reader in Religion and Gerontology.* 2nd ed. Chicago, IL: Exploration Press, 1985. 374p. $27.95; $13.95, paper. ISBN 0-913552-27-5; 0-913552-28-3, paper.

The editors of this anthology believe that churches and synagogues are a major social resource for meeting certain needs of the aging. It is in the hope of stimulating the thinking of the clergy, laity, and gerontologists about the resources available in religious institutions that they have compiled these writings on religion and gerontology. This collection will be of interest to those wishing to foster creative communication between the fields of religion and gerontology.

Monk, Abraham, ed. *Handbook of Gerontological Services.* New York: Van Nostrand Reinhold, 1985. 688p. $39.95. ISBN 0-442-27806-3.

Focusing on the everyday problems encountered by service professionals, this guide is a comprehensive review of the types of social intervention methods and the range of services available to the elderly today. All major service areas are covered from the aspects of need, assessment, intervention, theory, and policy. For gerontology students and professionals in the field, this handbook provides detailed information on the concerns and techniques of professional service practitioners, informal caregivers, community action groups, and other organizations involved with service to the elderly.

Rubenstein, Robert L. *Singular Paths: Old Men Living Alone.* New York: Columbia University Press, 1986. 265p. $30. ISBN 0-231-06206-0.

The author based this book on interviews with 47 single and widowed elderly males in Philadelphia. The study found many positive adaptations to living alone, including remaining in a self-owned house or renting an apartment. Attending senior-center activities was not important to many, leading the author to recommend that service providers expand center programs and outreach. This book is one of the few providing information on widowers and should be studied by service providers working with this population.

Sheehan, Susan. *Kate Quinton's Days.* New York: New American Library, 1985. Np. $3.95. ISBN 0-451-62423-8.

Sheehan, Pulitzer Prize winning author of *Is There No Place on Earth for Me?*, brings her reporting skills to the issues of health care and the aged through the personal account of Kate Quinton, an independent Irish woman trying to continue living within a community while undergoing multiple changes, most of them disabling. Sheehan describes the doctors, nurses, social workers, home attendants, and Medicaid officials who become part of Kate's existence. This important documentary is an illuminating view of health care services for the elderly.

Steinberg, Raymond M., and Genevieve W. Carter. *Case Management and the Elderly: A Handbook for Planning and Administering Programs.* Lexington, MA: Lexington Books, 1983. 224p. $35. ISBN 0-669-06089-5.

This handbook presents the subject of case management with the frail elderly from the perspective of the planner, the administrator, and the evaluator. The authors begin at the client level and discuss program planning from the viewpoint of the homebound elderly who will need services. There are suggested readings throughout the book to help the reader make informed choices. This was one of the first books written on case management and it is still an important work in the growing field of literature on the subject.

Tobin, Sheldon S., James W. Mellor, and Susan M. Anderson-Ray. *Enabling the Elderly: Religious Institutions within the Community Service System.* SUNY Series on Aging. Albany, NY: State University of New York Press, 1986. 192p. $39.50; $12.95, paper. ISBN 0-88706-334-9; 0-88706-335-7, paper.

For many people, churches and synagogues have been a constant in their lives that becomes even more important as they age. The authors demonstrate the importance of religion in the lives of older individuals, outline the nature of programming that can be conducted by churches and synagogues, and provide specific examples of the possibilities and problems in initiating service programs for the well, homebound, nursing home, and dying elderly. It is this detail of the problems as well as the possibilities of religious institutions working together with service agencies that makes this book most valuable.

Turock, Betty J. *Serving the Older Adult: A Guide to Library Programs and Information Services.* New York: Bowker, 1982. 294p. $34.95. ISBN 0-8352-1487-7.

Serving the Older Adult, a title in Bowker's Serving Special Populations Series, is designed to serve as a handbook for libraries and other information centers in starting or developing programs and services for older adults, their families, and other service providers. The author describes the older population and the history of library services to them and introduces some major theories of aging. The section on program planning, community analysis, citizen participation, staffing, and training leads into descriptions of model programs such as information and referral and lifelong learning and education. While the emphasis is on the public library, the final section, on information sources and bibliographies listing core references on aging, will enable other library professionals and older adults themselves to find additional information.

Vesperi, Maria D. *City of Green Benches: Growing Old in a New Downtown.* Ithaca, NY: Cornell University Press, 1985. 162p. $16.95; $8.95, paper. ISBN 0-8014-1818-6; 0-8014-9322-6, paper.

St. Petersburg, Florida, which once courted the elderly retiree, has recently sought, through urban renewal, to attract the young. The author examines the effect on the elderly of this attempt at rejuvenation by describing the conditions of older people's lives, the social programs created for them, and their interaction with the city around them. Vesperi considers the distorted image of old age, examines how new stereotypes have developed, and notes the contradiction between how the elderly see themselves and how they are seen by the community. This book will spark discussions of assumptions about old age.

Von Behren, Ruth. *Adult Day Care: A Program of Services for the Functionally Impaired.* Washington, DC: National Council on the Aging (NCOA), 1989. Np. $5.95. ISBN 0-910883-29-7.

This report provides an in-depth analysis of the national survey conducted by NCOA's National Institute on Adult Daycare. Included in the findings are relationships between licensing categories, funding sources, and participant and center characteristics, and an analysis of basic, professional, and service packages arranged by licensing category and major funding source. This report provides the most complete and up-to-date information available on adult daycare programs.

PERIODICALS

Journal of Gerontological Social Work. 4/yr. $36, individuals. $85, institutions. $132, libraries. Haworth Press, 10 Alice Street, Binghamton, NY 13904.

This journal is devoted to the study of social work theory and practice in the field of aging. It is directed toward the practice needs of social work administrators, practitioners, and supervisors in long-term care facilities, mental health centers, senior citizen centers, and public health agencies. Articles on topics such as elderly volunteers, group work with families of nursing home residents, and patterns of senior-center participation emphasize the applied aspects of gerontology that make this journal helpful.

Journal of Religion and Aging: The Interdisciplinary Journal of Practice, Theory, Applied Research. 4/yr. $28, individuals. $36, institutions. $60, libraries. Haworth Press, 10 Alice Street, Binghamton, NY 13904.

This journal is directed to religious professionals who work with the elderly, to secular professionals who work with the elderly and their families in religious institutions, and to the academic disciplines within the field of religion. Its goal is to inform these readers about developments in aging and the field of religious gerontology. Articles cover such topics as ethical problems in living will legislation; a comparison of Anglo and black congregations' use of networks for the aging; and religion, aging, and life satisfaction. There are signed book reviews. The journal is interfaith and multicultural and reflects the growing interest in aging and the human spirit.

Retirement

BOOKS

Dickinson, Peter A. *Retirement Edens outside the Sunbelt.* New York: E. P. Dutton, 1981. 288p. $15.50. ISBN 0-525-93174-0.

———. *Sunbelt Retirement.* New York: E. P. Dutton, 1978. Washington, DC: American Association of Retired Persons, 1987. 368p. $11.95. ISBN 0-673-248-32-1.

Dickinson's twin volumes rate a number of quality-of-life indicators, such as climate and environment, medical services, housing, cost of living, recreation and culture, and special senior services. It is clear that the author has spent time in all these places exploring, observing, and asking questions. He helps readers develop these skills by advising them where to go, whom to write or call (addresses and telephone numbers are provided), and what to ask. These are good guides for the retiree who is doing his or her own research on retirement locations.

Friedman, Roslyn, and Annette Nussbaum. *Coping with Your Husband's Retirement.* New York: Simon and Schuster, 1986. 223p. $6.95. ISBN 0-671-54719-4.

Now more than ever, men are living longer and retiring earlier. As a result, more and more couples are faced with years of being together 24 hours a day. The authors interviewed 75 wives of retirees. The women discuss the joys and frustrations of having a husband at home full-time and offer information on doing things together and separately, on planning travel, on avoiding friction over finances, and on adjusting to major moves. Couples will find this book a help in easing the transition into retirement.

Graebner, William. *A History of Retirement: The Meaning and Function of an American Institution, 1885-1978.* New Haven, CT: Yale University Press, 1980. 293p. OP; $12.95, paper. ISBN 0-300-02356-1; 03300-1, paper.

Based on primary sources, this book investigates such issues as the relationship of retirement to unemployment, changes in the conception of retirement in the twentieth century, and the development of Social Security. The author does not describe retirement legislation nor does he write much about how people have lived in retirement. This well-researched history of retirement will be of particular interest to historians, gerontologists, and political economists.

Howells, John. *Retirement Choices: For the Time of Your Life.* San Francisco, CA: Gateway Books, 1987. 348p. $10.95. ISBN 0-933469-03-9.

This guide is full of advice about housing, crime, cost of living, health, and social life, but it is very subjective. The author clearly is biased toward warm climates, prefers places where there is a variety of things to do and where interesting people live, and generally rejects the use of statistics. His emphasis is on making choices rather than on deciding where to go, and as a result he writes about possibilities that other guides do not even mention, such as "recreational vehicle" retirement, buying a farm, and joining the Peace Corps or a nudist colony. There is also an excellent chapter on retiring abroad. This is a book for someone thinking about lifestyle choices in retirement, for it offers a range of interesting possibilities to consider and includes enough information for readers to arrive at their own conclusions.

McClusky, Neil G., and Edgar F. Borgatta, eds. *Aging and Retirement: Prospects, Planning and Policy.* Beverly Hills, CA: Sage, 1981. 233p. $35; OP, paper. ISBN 0-8039-1756-2; 0-8039-1757-0, paper.

Written for policymakers, scholars, researchers, and specialists in the areas of social policy and gerontology, *Aging and Retirement* discusses the social, political, and economic prospects for the elderly retired in the United States. The contributors analyze health care, public processes governing retirement policies, redistribution of wealth, Social Security benefits, mandatory retirement, pensions, and special programs for women. This book will shed light and foster discussion on laws and issues directly related to retirement.

Milletti, Mario A. *Voices of Experience: 1500 Retired People Talk about Retirement.* New York: Teachers Insurance and Annuity Association, 1985. Rev ed. 208p. $3, paper. ISBN 0-9613704-1-6.

This book is about the personal retirement experiences of TIAA-CREF (Teacher's Insurance and Annuity Association–College Retirement Equities Fund) annuitants. It presents the suggestions and observations of the already retired for the benefit of the retired-to-be. *Voices of Experience* covers such concerns as finances, health and housing, adjustment, altered relations with one's spouse, and retirement as a single person. Although all these retirees are from academia, this does not limit the usefulness of the information. This is a valuable resource to anyone who is thinking ahead to retirement.

Palder, Edward L. *The Retirement Sourcebook: Your Complete Guide to Health, Leisure, and Consumer Information.* Kensington, OH: Woodbine House, 1989. 350p. $14.95. ISBN 0-933149-24-7.

This is a compendium of information on a variety of subjects of interest to those planning active retirement lifestyles. Readers can find lists of brochures available on buying apartment insurance and catalogs of mail-order pet supplies as well as information on how to request presidential birthday greetings. Also included is information on health care and crime prevention volunteer programs. There are lists of telephone hotlines, publications, and clearinghouses. This book has an easy-to-read format and is a wonderful reference tool.

Sherman, Michael. *The Retirement Account Calculator: Complete Savings and Withdrawal Tables for IRA and Keogh Plans.* Chicago, IL: Contemporary Books, 1986. 284p. OP. ISBN 0-8092-5002-0.

This book is directed toward consumers who prefer to place their IRAs in fixed-rate savings investments. It is designed as a tool to help investors compare investments with differing interest rates and solve a variety of mathematical problems associated with such investments. The book is organized in an easy-to-use format, and no advanced mathematical skills are necessary. It provides answers for the often-asked questions: How much can I withdraw each month after I retire? How long will my "nest egg" last at different rates of withdrawal?

Weaver, Peter, and Annette Buchanan. *What To Do with What You've Got: The Practical Guide to Money Management in Retirement.* 2nd ed. Washington, DC: American Association of Retired Persons and Scott, Foresman, 1989. 210p. $7.95. ISBN 0-673-24805-4.

Financial columnist Peter Weaver and consumer educator Annette Buchanan provide advice and information on setting your life goals; what you should know about retiring to a smaller, more manageable home or to a retirement community; how it pays to review your insurance options; and how to keep health problems and their attendant costs at bay. This book provides sound advice to those looking toward retirement as well as to those already retired.

Sexuality

BOOKS

Brecher, Edward M. *Love, Sex, and Aging: A Consumer Union Report.* Boston, MA: Little, Brown, 1986. 441p. $12.95, paper. ISBN 0-326-10719-0.

This report is a comprehensive study of the sexual attitudes and activities of Americans over 50, prepared by the Consumer's Union with data collected from 4,246 men and women in response to detailed questionnaires. Although the respondents do not comprise a representative sample of the U.S. population (the sample is limited to readers of *Consumer Reports*), this does not detract from the practical information and sound advice given on sexuality in the later years. Numerous life stories and quotations are used throughout the book, affirming that life can be highly enjoyable and sexually fulfilling after 50.

Butler, Robert N., and Myrna I. Lewis. *Love and Sex after 40: A Guide for Men and Women for Their Mid and Later Years.* Santa Barbara, CA: ABC-CLIO, 1987. 202p. $19.95. ISBN 1-55736-008-1.

An updated and expanded version of the 1976 classic *Sex after 60*, this volume is useful both for lay readers over 40 and for the professionals who counsel them. The book's strongest asset is its commonsense view of sex and aging. The authors present medical and scientific evidence about the effects of stress, illness, disability, drugs, and certain surgeries on sexuality; provide insight on communicating with a spouse; and furnish listings throughout of organizations and resource materials for the reader who wants more detailed information. This book is also available in large print.

———. *Love and Sex after 60* (rev. ed. of *Sex after 60*, 1976). New York: Harper & Row, 1988. 191p. $16.95. ISBN 0-06-055125-9.

In this revision of their landmark book *Sex after 60*, the authors continue to explore the social, medical, and psychological problems relating to the sex lives of men and women over 60. They debunk the myth that most sexual problems are psychological in origin and present the latest information on diagnostic and surgical procedures, the role of illnesses such as diabetes in sexual problems, the effects of drugs and alcohol, and other medical considerations. The authors also show the need for loving relationships until the end of life. The public, the professions, and older people will find much in this book to challenge existing negative stereotypes of aging.

Schover, Leslie R. *Prime Time: Sexual Health for Men over Fifty.* New York: Holt, Rinehart and Winston, 1984. 254p. OP. ISBN 0-03-064028-8.

Despite a rapidly accumulating body of research showing that male sexual capacities are more modest than myth would have it, this medical knowledge about male sexuality is not reaching the public. In particular, men over 50 need this information to help them and their partners form realistic expectations about their sexual relationships. This guide covers such topics as what women really want, common diseases of aging and their sexual effects, and medical treatments like penile senile prosthesis and hormone therapy. Written by a practicing clinical psychologist who treats patients with sexual concerns, this is a self-help book suited for the general public as well as for therapists and counselors.

Starr, Bernard D., and Marcella Baker Weiner. *The Starr-Weiner Report on Sex and Sexuality in the Mature Years.* New York: McGraw-Hill, 1981. 302p. $5.95, paper. ISBN 0-07-060878-4.

This landmark study of sexual activities in men and women over the age of 60 puts paid to the widely held belief that most people have little or no sex life after 60. The authors interview more than 800 people from 60 to 91 who reveal that sex is as good now as when they were younger. This well-conducted study will erase the myths and misinformation that have grown around the idea of old-age sexuality. While helpful to the professionals who work in the field, this book will be encouraging to older people and to the middle-aged who can look forward to spending a quarter of their lifespan beyond the age of 60.

Weg, Ruth B., ed. *Sexuality in the Later Years: Roles and Behavior.* New York: Academic Press, 1983. 299p. $29.50. ISBN 0-12-741320-0.

A significant gap exists between the reality of sexuality in the later years and the stereotypes of "dirty old men" and "dirty old women" that persist in society. This volume explores human sexuality from a perspective beyond that of intercourse and presents evidence from anthropology, psychology, physiology, and sociology to prove that the topic is multidimensional. The research concentrates on options, possibilities, and potentials for the individualization of sex roles and sexual behavior of older persons. Researchers, scholars, and policymakers as well as health care providers will find this book helpful in the effort to eradicate ageism.

FILM AND VIDEOCASSETTE

The Search for Intimacy: Love, Sex and Relationships in the Later Years

Type: 16mm film, ½" VHS and Beta videocassette, color
Length: 25 min.
Date: 1986
Cost: Purchase $450, rental $50
Source: Perennial Education, Inc.
          930 Pitner
          Evanston, IL 60202

Hosted by Alex Comfort, *The Search for Intimacy* is a montage in which a variety of married, single, widowed, and divorced older people speak about the nature and importance of intimate relationships in their lives. They provide viewers with an accurate glimpse of the range of relationships that are meaningful to older people. Subjects include an 87-year-old widowed man, a 63-year-old single woman, a couple who have been married 52 years, and a 62-year-old divorced woman. This film is intended for an audience of older people and would serve as a discussion-starter for senior citizens' groups.

Technology

BOOKS AND GOVERNMENT PUBLICATIONS

Dunkle, Ruth E., Marie R. Haug, and Marvin Rosenberg. *Communications Technology and the Elderly: Issues and Forecasts.* New York: Springer, 1984. 238p. $31. ISBN 0-8261-4060-2.

An outcome of a symposium held at Case Western Reserve in 1981, this is a reflective, insightful compilation of reports on communication devices and their real or perceived impact on individuals. Included are aids for those with impaired vision or hearing and "aged-user-friendly" mechanisms designed to connect the elderly with health care delivery systems, recreation, and education. The authors point out that in our avid search for technologies to lengthen life and compensate for disabilities, we overlook the human dimension. They warn us that we must seek input from elderly users in the planning, development, and implementation of technology. Theorists and inventors as well as the elderly user can benefit from this realistic analysis of the multidimensional world of technology and aging.

La Buda, Dennis R., ed. *The Gadget Book: Ingenious Devices for Easier Living.* Washington, DC: American Association of Retired Persons, 1987. 160p. $10.95. ISBN 0-673-24819-4.

This guidebook was a project of the American Society on Aging and describes devices for easier everyday living. It includes the areas of personal care, home environment, home maintenance, communications, mobility, health care, and leisure and recreation. More than 300 products are described, and listings include black-and-white photos, cost, and the names of the manufacturers and distributors. This book will prove helpful to anyone of any age who needs assistance with daily tasks.

Lesnoff-Caravaglia, Gari. *Aging in a Technological Society.* Vol. 6 of Frontiers in Aging. New York: Human Sciences Press, 1988. 301p. $36.95. ISBN 0-89885-382-6.

The author addresses issues of technology and aging that are of current concern and that will grow in scope and magnitude in the future. The book ranges from theory to methods of adapting various technologies to meet practical needs of the elderly. The contributors are from academia, the health care community, industry, and government agencies, and they put into perspective areas of health care technology that can meet the needs of the elderly. They also point out technologies that have failed, and it is the latter discussion that will help those trying to develop technology for the future.

McGuire, Francis A., ed. *Computer Technology and the Aged.* New York: Haworth Press, 1986. 119p. $24.95. ISBN 0-86656-481-0. (Also published as *Activities, Adaptation and Aging* Vol. 8, No. 1.)

The papers included in this publication discuss ways to use computers in activity programs for older individuals and ways to incorporate the newest technology in the delivery of services to older adults. Articles include information on the use of computers in assessment, in education, and with brain injured individuals and information that will be useful to computer novices. This book is one of the few resources available to assist activity personnel in designing programs that take advantage of computer technology.

Phillips, Alice H., and Caryl K. Roman. *A Practical Guide to Independent Living for Older People.* Seattle, WA: Pacific Search Press, 1984. 140p. $6.95. ISBN 0-914718-92-4.

Easy-to-hold tableware, flashing telephone signals, grab bars, and close-captioned television decoders are just a few of the many products and services that can make life easier and safer for some elderly people. Yet, countless older people will not use them because they view such products as symbols of aging. This book describes many handy devices and discusses their advantages in an easy-going, positive tone. The author states that we can all work to change attitudes and eliminate the stigma by encouraging people to see assistive aids as tools that allow independence, rather than as emblems of dependent old age. An appendix includes a list of supply houses and catalogs.

U.S. Congress, Office of Technology Assessment. *Technology and Aging in America.* Washington, DC: Government Printing Office, 1985. 496p. OP. Stock No. 0-52-003-00970-6.

This study focuses on the functional status of the elderly and ways in which technology can assist them to maintain their independence and enhance their quality of life. The report stresses the need for a coordinated approach to long-term care and for improved technologies to assess health and functional status. The housing and living environments of the elderly are considered, as is the impact of changes in workplace technology. Those working with older people in the workplace, the home, the health care setting, and the community will find food for thought in this report on technological changes and the challenge of applying those changes for the benefit of the older population.

PERIODICAL

International Journal of Technology & Aging. 2/yr. $24, individuals. $54, institutions. Human Sciences Press, 233 Spring Street, New York, NY 10013-1578.

As people live longer, we have come to realize that technology helps the process, as well as ensures that most will lead more or less active lives. This journal is concerned with explaining technologies to assist the elderly that are currently emerging from government research in the fields of sensory loss, robotics, and lifestyles for longevity. Most of the contributors are involved with coordinating and leading programs for the aged, which makes for a practical, highly pragmatic view of this major subject.

Wellness and Fitness

BOOKS

Butler, Robert N., and Herbert L. Gleason, eds. *Productive Aging: Enhancing Vitality in Later Life.* New York: Springer, 1985. 176p. $25.95. ISBN 0-8261-4810-7.

The contributors to this book address the topic of the relationships among aging, productivity, and health. How can older people continue to work, to participate, to volunteer, and to maintain and promote their own health and self-care? How do we orient our attention toward productivity rather than dependency? The authors, representing several countries and cultures, develop a plan of action designed to shatter stereotypes and focus on issues affecting any nation's elderly.

Chernoff, Ronni, and David A. Lipschitz, eds. *Health Promotion and Disease Prevention in the Elderly.* Vol. 35 of Aging Series. New York: Raven Press, 1988. 204p. $69. ISBN 0-88167-390-0.

A partial solution to the problem of the growing need for health care services for the elderly is to emphasize health promotion and disease prevention programs for the elderly population. This collection of papers examines some of the current knowledge and research about health promotion and disease prevention activities, including the areas of nutrition and exercise.

Christensen, Alice, and David Rankin. *Easy Does It: Yoga for Older People.* San Francisco, CA: Harper & Row, 1979. 112p. $11.95. ISBN 0-06-250145-3.

This is a specialized daily program of yoga exercise, breathing, meditation, philosophy, and nutrition for older people. There are clear, step-by-step illustrations in the book, which has a spiral binding so it will lie flat for easy referral while readers are exercising. Each section has photographs of real people doing the exercises along with quotations from them as to the program's effectiveness. This manual can be used by the elderly exercising at home by themselves or by yoga instructors and health care professionals working with older adults.

de Vries, Herbert A., and Dianne Hales. *Fitness after 50*. New York: Scribners, 1982. 151p. $12.95. ISBN 0-684-17485-5.

Believing that it is never too late to be fit, the authors present a simple, self-administered exercise regimen that can be followed by older people who have been out of shape for years. With clear illustrations of how each exercise is done, tables showing the amount of exercise appropriate for people at varying levels of fitness, and charts for keeping track of one's progress, the authors' combination of walking, jogging, and simple calisthenics provides a complete exercise program for men and women over 50.

Dychtwald, Ken, ed. *Wellness and Health Promotion for the Elderly*. Rockville, MD: Aspen Systems Corp., 1986. 378p. $39.50. ISBN 0-87189-238-3.

Health promotion for older people comes as a surprise to those who link efforts at health promotion and disease prevention with the earlier years of life. Given the continued advances in life expectancy, however, it behooves us to do more to ensure that we live out our longer lives with full mental and physical health. The contributors to this book suggest that exercise, proper diet and nutrition, stress management, and wise health consumerism, among other things, can help the older person as well as the young person. Health professionals, activity directors, and seniors will find the suggested health promotion programs valuable.

Flatten, Kay, Barbara Wilhite, and Eleanor Reyes-Watson, eds. *Exercise Activities for the Elderly*. Vol. 19 of Springer Series on Adulthood and Aging. New York: Springer, 1988. 206p. $21.95. ISBN 0-8261-5910-9.

This manual is one of a two-volume set that includes a companion book, *Recreation Activities for the Elderly*. Part one includes the information needed by the recreational leader to use the exercises effectively—understanding aging and the needs of the frail elderly as well as methods for working with such individuals. Part two presents the exercises, which are organized into interest areas—strength, arthritis, diabetes, Parkinson's disease, and special purposes such as bladder control and in-bed flexibility. The manual includes suggestions of audiovisuals and illustrations of each exercise. Extremely useful for those working directly with institutionalized and homebound elders.

———. *Recreation Activities for the Elderly.* Vol. 20 of Springer Series on Adulthood and Aging. New York: Springer, 1988. 226p. $21.95. ISBN 0-8261-6030-1.

The second of a two-volume set, this easy-to-follow guide presents a wide range of recreational activities appropriate for homebound and institutionalized elderly. Following the same format as *Exercise Activities for the Elderly,* this volume includes simple crafts; hobbies focusing on collections, nature, and the arts; and games emphasizing both mental and physical activity. Both books are designed to be used by staff or volunteers who lead activity programs for frail older persons.

Gordon, Michael. *Old Enough To Feel Better: A Medical Guide for Seniors.* Baltimore, MD: Johns Hopkins University Press, 1989. Rev. ed. 400p. $14.95. ISBN 0-8018-3807-X.

Gordon argues that the older population should not accept the stereotypical notion that old age is inevitably linked to disability and dysfunction. He explains the common problems, both medical and social, that affect the older person and asserts that it is never too late to reverse poor health habits or diminish the effects of the aging process. In part one Gordon shows how to take an active interest in one's health. Part two is a reference guide to common complaints, with descriptions of symptoms and diagnoses that will help readers understand how the body works. This book will give seniors an understanding of their health needs and enable them to make maximum use of health services.

Kart, Cary S., and Seamus P. Metress. *Nutrition, the Aged, and Society.* Englewood Cliffs, NJ: Prentice-Hall, 1984. 212p. OP. ISBN 0-13-627521-4.

This book will serve as an introductory text to the role of nutrition in the aging process. Several of the major theories of biological aging include nutrition as one mechanism involved in the process of aging. Nutrition also plays a part in the course of many degenerative diseases. As well, food may be important to the elderly for social-psychological reasons. Its relevance to these diverse areas of gerontology makes this text suitable for students of nursing, medicine, health education, social work, psychology, and home economics as well as for allied health professionals.

Kemper, Donald W., et al., eds. *Growing Younger Handbook*. 2nd ed. Boise, ID: Healthwise, Inc., 1986. 133p. $10. ISBN 0-9612690-7-3.

While we cannot change our chronological age, we can reduce our health age by staying physically fit, eating well, relaxing, and maintaining a positive self-attitude. This handbook is a self-guided program for older adults interested in improving their health. The chapters on health care management and medical self-care have diagrams, tests, sample forms, charts, and reading lists to help the reader practice the suggested skills and activities. This is a basic guide to help older people improve their health on a day-to-day basis.

Lesnoff-Caravaglia, Gari, ed. *Handbook of Applied Gerontology*. New York: Human Sciences Press, 1987. 460p. $49.95. ISBN 0-8988-5314-1.

This book is focused around the underlying themes of prevention and intervention in the overall health care of older persons. By reviewing the physical changes, mental health, and social realities of old age, the contributors conclude that the multidisciplinary approach to old age is of singular importance. As we age, we change in idiosyncratic ways along physical, mental, and social dimensions, and the needs associated with these interrelated changes must be recognized. This volume provides essential information to practitioners, researchers, students, and professionals involved in policymaking on aging or in delivery of health care services. It would also lend itself well as a text for upper-level courses in social work and gerontology.

Ley, Olga. *Exercises for Non-Athletes over Fifty-One*. New York: Schocken Books, 1985. 98p. $12.95. ISBN 0-8052-3979-0.

The author has been teaching exercise for over 40 years and her followers, like herself, have gotten older. Viewing exercise for the elderly from her aged vantage point, she recommends a routine emphasizing movement and flexibility, not just technical exercises. The exercises are simple, can be done at home (she calls some "sneaky" because one can sneak them into any daily activity), and do not require any special equipment. The book's tone is light and optimistic. Exercises are illustrated by the author. Older people who are put off exercise by the sight of a 110-pound young thing in a leotard doing things that are impossible for an older person will find help in this book.

Linkletter, Art. *Old Age Is Not for Sissies: Choices for Senior Americans.* New York: Viking, 1987. 256p. $17.95. ISBN 0-670-81922-0.

With good sense and humor, performer Linkletter addresses problems and preoccupations of the elderly. Determinedly upbeat, Linkletter offers advice on health and medical care, housing, finances, family relations, and loneliness. He suggests that constructive options open to the aging include developing new interests, serving others, and participating in group projects and social activities. The author also discusses his plans to form a national program of public education to reach 55 million senior Americans. The book is full of examples of famous older achievers—such as Norman Vincent Peale and the Reagans—and will appeal to seniors who are healthy, active, and independent.

Ostrow, Andrew C. *Physical Activity and the Older Adult: Psychological Perspectives.* Princeton, NJ: Princeton Book Co., 1984. 175p. $14.95. ISBN 0-9166-228-2.

This book explores the myths and realities of physical activity for the older adult. The emphasis is on evaluating the scientific evidence concerning the impact of physical activity on the physical and mental health of the older adult. Ostrow deplores the tendency to disengage from physical activity as one grows older and discusses the need for and training of physical activity leaders for older adults. This is an appropriate textbook for students in psychology, physical education, social work, and nursing and for those who are preparing to become leaders of older-adult physical activity programs.

Ralston, Jeannie. *Walking for the Health of It: The Easy and Effective Exercise for People over 50.* Washington, DC: American Association of Retired Persons, 1986. 212p. $6.95. ISBN 0-673-24826-7.

This is a "how-to" guide for those interested in the health and fitness benefits of walking. The author, a health and fitness writer, gives advice and information on how to get maximum health benefits from walking, how to choose the right shoes and other gear, and how to design a personal walking program. There is also an appendix containing names and addresses of equipment and clothing manufacturers and suggested exercises to supplement the walking program.

Ross, Mary Alice. *Fitness for the Aging Adult with Visual Impairment: An Exercise and Resource Manual.* New York: American Foundation for the Blind, 1984. 84p. $8.95. ISBN 0-89128-125-8.

We now know that even a small amount of exercise can help an older person fight the ailments, disabilities, and frailty of old age. Typical exercise, however, may not be possible for those whose mobility is restricted because of visual impairment. This manual sets out the types of exercises that can be used by visually impaired elders and provides lists of guidelines and necessary equipment along with photographs of older adults doing the exercises. This practical exercise manual will help older persons, their family members, and therapists who work with the elderly.

Rossman, Isadore. *Looking Forward: The Complete Medical Guide to Successful Aging.* New York: E. P. Dutton, 1989. 608p. $22.95. ISBN 0-525-24785-8.

Rossman has written a comprehensive, easy-to-use medical guide for those 50 or older. He includes practical advice on sensible nutrition, protecting against hardening of the arteries, dealing with diabetes, avoiding accidents, use of nonprescription drugs, and more. The text is punctuated with "Key Fact" and "Health Report" boxes that provide usable and up-to-date information on important medical developments, procedures, and terms. This is an excellent new addition to the literature on personal health.

Skinner, B. F., and Margaret E. Vaughan. *Enjoying Old Age: A Program of Self-Management.* New York: W. W. Norton, 1983. 157p. OP. ISBN 0-393-01805-9.

B. F. Skinner, noted psychologist and 79-year-old senior citizen, has written a "how-to" guide for taking charge of one's old age. He insists we can adjust to our everyday world as we age and enjoy more of it. Printed in large type, the book gives specific advice on aging, with some main points being: learn to relax, keep busy, maintain a sense of humor, take steps to deal with physical frailties, stay attractive, and maintain our dignity. This small, practical guide suggests that we can manage our environment and live a long time without being old.

Thornton, Howard A. *A Medical Handbook for Senior Citizens and Their Families.* Dover, MA: Auburn House, 1989. 350p. $29.95; $16.95, paper. ISBN 0-86569-171-1; 0-86569-175-4, paper.

This highly readable book opens with chapters on the diagnosis and treatment of such medical problems as heart disease, cancer, stroke, and sensory loss. Thornton goes on to address prevention with excellent overviews of diet, smoking, drinking, exercise, the complete physical, and immunizations of the elderly (a generally overlooked subject). The book ends with lists of resources and agencies; information on support systems; and lists of foods high in sodium, calcium, purines, and iron. This handbook will give family caregivers and older adults a good overview of the medical aspects of aging.

PERIODICALS

Age Page. Irregular. Free. National Institute on Aging, Information Center, P.O. Box 8057, Gaithersberg, MD 20898-8057.

This irregular publication provides a quick, practical look at some of the health topics that interest older people. It appears as single sheets printed in large type and in lay language. Easily available and well written, *Age Pages* deal with such topics as "Accidents and the Elderly," "Dealing with Diabetes," "When You Need a Nursing Home," and "Skin Care and Aging." Certain titles are also available in Chinese or Spanish. The general public and older adults will find these brief but authoritative pages useful.

Healthy Older People Program Memo. 12/yr. Free. Health Advocacy Services, Program Department, AARP, 1909 K Street, NW, Washington, DC 20049; (202) 728-4476.

"Healthy Older People" is a national public campaign to educate older people about health practices that can reduce risks of disabling illness. The program encourages older adults to improve their health by eating right, using medicines safely, exercising regularly, and preventing injuries. This newsletter was designed for program planners and focuses on health promotion and aging. Each issue presents one or more innovative programs that can serve as models for anyone planning health promotion programs at the local or state level.

FILMS AND VIDEOCASSETTES

Be Well: The Later Years
Type: Four 16mm films, ½" VHS videocassettes, color
Length: 24 min. each
Date: 1983
Cost: Film purchase $1695 series, $450 each, rental $100;
½" VHS purchase $1195 series, $315 each, rental $100

Source: Churchill Films
662 North Robertson Boulevard
Los Angeles, CA 90069-9990

This series of four films contains health information for older people given by authorities who devote themselves to helping others live healthy lives. Hosted by a fit and energetic Milton Berle, the films present older people who have reaped the benefits of living healthy lives. The advice is made painless through the use of comedy vignettes that make older adults smile while they are being motivated. The four films are *Health in the Later Years, Nutrition in the Later Years, Physical Fitness in the Later Years,* and *Stress in the Later Years.*

Don't Take It Easy
Type: 16mm film, ½" VHS and Beta videocassette, color
Length: 20 min.
Date: 1985
Cost: Film purchase $500, rental $55; ½" VHS or Beta purchase $450, rental $55
Source: Filmmaker's Library
133 East 58th Street
New York, NY 10022

Don't Take It Easy is well suited to the employee approaching retirement or to any person over age 40 who is not participating in a regular fitness program. Personal examples of various fitness plans and options are presented. Swimming, tai chi, walking, and joining an exercise class are a few of the suggestions demonstrated to show the viewer how high levels of physical and mental health can be maintained. This film would be useful to the student who is preparing to work with older adults in planning activities as well as to the middle-income, urban adult who is planning retirement.

Keep Movin': Fitness for Older Adults
Type: ½" VHS videocassette, color
Length: 27 min.
Date: 1985
Cost: Purchase $225, rental $35
Source: Grandview Hospital
c/o Mediatech
110 West Hubbard Street
Chicago, IL 60620

This program demonstrates easy exercises to upbeat music, providing older people with a simple and enjoyable model for staying active. Participants of all levels of ability, including those who are wheelchair-bound, are encouraged to go at their own pace with moderate regular exercise, using every joint every day.

Staying Active: Wellness after Sixty
Type: 16mm film, ½" VHS and Beta videocassette, color
Length: 28 min.
Date: 1986
Cost: $495, free preview
Source: Spectrum Films, Inc.
2755 Jefferson Street, Suite 103
Carlsbad, CA 92008

Staying Active is an overview of health and lifestyle issues for seniors. It features people in their sixties, seventies, and eighties who are leading active lives by optimizing their physical and emotional health. Many are bouncing back from the setbacks that often accompany older age. Through their examples, they encourage viewers to make positive choices in the areas of nutrition, stress management, exercise, and involvement with others.

Women

BOOKS

Alexander, Jo, et al., eds. *Women and Aging: An Anthology by Women.* Corvallis, OR: Calyx Books, 1986. 264p. $12. ISBN 0-934971-00-5.

This anthology of prose, poetry, fiction, photography, and art provides beautiful proof of the consequences of growing older. Voices of old women and of some women not so old celebrate age and at the same time document the ageism inherent in being elderly and female.

Coyle, Jean M., comp. *Women and Aging: A Selected Annotated Bibliography.* No. 9 of Bibliographies and Indexes in Gerontology. New York: Greenwood Press, 1989. 135p. $35.95. ISBN 0-313-26021-4.

Focusing on women and the aging process, this bibliography cites books and journal articles published between 1980 and early 1988. The major areas covered include roles and relationships, economics, employment, retirement, health, sexuality, religion, housing, racial and ethnic groups, policy issues, international concerns, and middle age.

Doress, Paula Brown, et al. *Ourselves, Growing Older: Women Aging with Knowledge and Power.* New York: Simon and Schuster, 1987. 576p. $24.95; $15.95, paper. ISBN 0-671-50501-7; 0-671-64424-6, paper.

The Boston Women's Health Book Collective and the Midlife and Older Women Book Project have produced an outstanding work focusing on the health, social, and psychological concerns of women in midlife and beyond. Chapters cover such topics as birth control and childbearing in middle age, which are omitted in many women's health manuals. Other topics include diet, health habits, family relationships, housing, retirement, money, and caregiving as well as major medical problems from arthritis to memory lapse and loss. There is a comprehensive resource list. This second generation of the landmark book *Our Bodies, Ourselves* encourages women 40 or older to take control of their health care.

Fisher, Lucy Rose. *Linked Lives: Adult Daughters and Their Mothers.* New York: Harper & Row, 1986. 238p. $17.95. ISBN 0-06-091412-2.

In *Linked Lives* the author analyzes the emotionally charged relationships between mothers and their daughters. It identifies two key turning points in the mother-daughter relationship: when the daughter becomes a mother herself and when the mother becomes frail. The mother-daughter bond varies from one family to the next. But the mother's role as primary caregiver in most families is passed on from mother to daughter and thus is carried on generation after generation. Fisher has written this book for professionals and for mothers and daughters who would like to learn more about their relationship with one another.

Foehner, Charlotte, and Carol Cozart. *The Widow's Handbook: A Guide for Living.* Golden, CO: Fulcrum, 1988. 301p. $18.95; $14.95, paper. ISBN 1-55591-014-9; 1-55591-023-8, paper.

Both authors draw on their own widowhood in trying to prepare others for this stressful time when crucial financial and legal decisions must be made. They cover both the emotional as well as the practical (legal, tax, and pension/benefits) issues facing a widow. They also include timelines for completing important matters, sample forms, checksheets, and detailed instructions on nearly every financial eventuality. This comprehensive guide will help widows specifically during the two years following their loss.

Grambs, Jean D. *Women over 40.* 2nd ed. New York: Springer, 1989. 288p. $35.95. ISBN 0-8261-1300-2X.

Revised and updated, this readable book presents information from recent research about older women. *Women over 40* challenges erroneous stereotypes of women in the aging years in such diverse areas as health, sexuality, work, and retirement. This well-organized text would be of interest to those in gerontology, human development, and women's studies.

Painter, Charlotte. *Gifts of Age.* San Francisco, CA: Chronicle Books, 1985. 147p. $16.95. ISBN 0-87701-368-3.

These portraits and essays of 32 remarkable women are a fascinating insight into just how productive one's extended life can be. All of the women in this book are more than 65 years of age, including such well-known personalities as Julia Child, M. F. K. Fisher, and Joan Baez, Senior. The gifts of age referred to in the title are the time, the freedom, and the wisdom to develop new images of oneself, and these essays and photographs will help anyone face the aging process with more cheer. This book should be read by young and old and will provide inspiration for exploring new challenges in the mature years.

Porcino, Jane. *Growing Older, Getting Better: A Handbook for Women in the Second Half of Life.* Reading, MA: Addison-Wesley, 1983. 364p. OP; $12.95, paper. ISBN 0-201-05593-7; 0-201-05592-9, paper.

This important book for midlife women is a comprehensive sourcebook that covers changing roles, physical aging, health concerns, housing, and discrimination. Included are references to materials and resource organizations and illustrations. The author offers information and encouraging advice on menopause; grandmotherhood; major health threats such as osteoporosis, diabetes, and cardiovascular ailments; and sexuality and intimacy—essential information that older women need to achieve maximum good health.

Seskin, Jane. *Alone—Not Lonely: Independent Living for Women over Fifty.* Washington, DC: American Association of Retired Persons and Scott, Foresman, 1985. 228p. $6.95. ISBN 0-673-24814-3.

Written for women living alone, whether single, widowed, or divorced, this book offers advice and encouragement. *Alone—Not Lonely* contains lists of resources (books, organizations, and toll-free hotlines) and guidance to help with the physical, emotional, and social adjustments a single woman faces. Topics covered include how to get over the anger experienced at being alone; how to secure credit, earn money, find a job, or go back to school; and how to change the scene by moving to a new place. This practical book with its information and suggestions can help single women over 50 learn to live better.

PERIODICALS

Broomstick: By, for & about Women over Forty. 6/yr. $15. 3543 18th Street, San Francisco, CA 94110.

Broomstick is a national feminist, reader-participation publication. It accepts submissions only from women who are over 40. There are book reviews and advertisements for merchandise and services for women over 40. *Broomstick* was chosen as a title because it represents skills—homemaking and paid jobs—and change—the new broom sweeps clean.

Hot Flash: A Newsletter for Midlife and Older Women. 4/yr. $25. National Action Forum for Midlife and Older Women, SUNY–Stony Brook, Box 816, Stony Brook, NY 11790-1609.

This newsletter addresses the general health and social concerns of both midlife and older women. Recent articles written by women professionals have explored sexuality, health and medical problems of older women, pros and cons of estrogen replacement therapy, and physical and mental health insurance for women over 40. The print is large and readable. *Hot Flash* is designed to be of interest to all women and to those dealing with women, aging, and health.

FILM AND VIDEOCASSETTE

Acting Our Age
Type: 16mm film, ½" VHS videocassette, color
Length: 58 min.
Date: 1988
Cost: Film purchase $895, rental $85; ½" VHS purchase $250, rental $85

Source: Direct Cinema Limited
           P.O. Box 69799
           Los Angeles, CA 90069

The viewer is treated to vignettes of six women ages 65 to 74 who share their insights on their own aging process, their rage concerning the association of age with ugliness and evil, the loss of friends, the need to skimp and save, and the patronizing attitude of the "helping" professions. None of these women is merely coping. They give meaning to the importance of making choices and of having choices to make. Because this film is sensitive without being maudlin, it should be a useful tool in heightening younger audiences' awareness of aging and will also serve those who are facing age-related changes in their own lives.

Index

AARP Pharmacy Service Prescription Drug Handbook, 88
About Mourning: Support and Guidance for the Bereaved, 56
Abstracts in Social Gerontology: Current Literature on Aging, 28
Abuse, 24, 37, 48, 66–68
   in nursing homes, 108
Achenbaum, Andrew W., 29
Acting Our Age, 152–153
Activities, Adaptation and Aging, 139
Activities Handbook and Instructor's Guide for Expanding Options for Older Adults with Developmental Disabilities, 79
Adapting Successfully to Parkinson's Disease, 91
Aday, Ron H., 66
Addiction, 38–40
   See also Alcoholism; Drug abuse
Administration on Aging, 15, 37
Adult children, 47–49, 50, 52, 53
   See also Care of elderly; Families
Adult Day Care: A Program of Services for the Functionally Impaired, 132
Adult daycare. See Daycare
Advance Data from Vital and Health Statistics, 39, 80
Advocacy, 50
After Ninety, 31
Age discrimination, 36, 37, 60, 151
   See also Ageism
Age, Health, and Employment, 68
Age or Need? Public Policies for Older People, 124
Age Page, 147
Age stratification, 29
Age Wave: The Challenges and Opportunities of an Aging America, 32

Ageing International, 36
Ageism, 115, 121, 138, 149
   See also Age discrimination
Ageline, 17, 24
Agencies, 22, 24, 27
   area, 25
   federal, 15–17, 32, 37
   housing, 98–99
   local, 15
   state, 15, 25
Aging
   alteration of, 35
   attitudes toward, 29, 33
   and attractiveness, 38
   challenges of, 116
   meaning of, 31
   perceptions about, 32, 33
   of population, 69, 72
   positive images of, 103, 131, 145, 146, 151
   process of, 22, 34, 118, 143, 149
   and productivity, 141
   status of, 23, 29, 34
   theories of, 131
   trends in, 23, 31–33, 36, 51
Aging: A Guide to Resources, 21
The Aging Adult in Children's Books and Nonprint Media: An Annotated Bibliography, 105
Aging America: Trends and Projections, 23
Aging and Behavior, 30
Aging and Mental Health, 115
Aging and Rehabilitation, 74
Aging and Retirement: Prospects, Planning and Policy, 134
Aging and Sensory Change: An Annotated Bibliography, 92
Aging and the Human Spirit: A Reader in Religion and Gerontology, 129

Index

Aging and the Product Environment, 99–100
The Aging Employee, 71
The Aging Enterprise, 122
The Aging Eye: A Guide for Nurses, 93
Aging in a Technological Society, 139
Aging in the Eighties: America in Transition, 33
The Aging Network: Programs and Services, 128–129
Aging Network News, 36
The Aging Population in the Twenty-First Century: Statistics for Health Policy, 123
Aging Research & Training, 37
Aging, the Ethnic Factor, 119–120
Aging with a Disability, 92
An Aging World, 35
AIDS, 56
Alcohol, 40–42, 137, 147
Alcohol and Drug Abuse in Old Age, 40
Alcohol and Old Age, 41
Alcoholism, 40–42, 118–119
Alexander, Jo, 149
Aliki, 103
All about Medicare, 61–62
Alone—Not Lonely: Independent Living for Women over Fifty, 151–152
Altman, Maya, 58
Alzheimer's disease, 13, 23, 42, 43
 coping with, 117–118
 and family, 43–46, 49, 53, 86, 104
 and home care, 95, 96, 102
 living arrangements for, 113
 public policy on, 43
 research on, 45
 support services for, 42, 44
 symptoms of, 42, 45, 46
 treatment of, 42–45
Alzheimer's Disease and Related Disorders Association, 13
American Association for International Aging, 13, 27
American Association of Homes for the Aging, 13
American Association of Retired Persons, 12, 17, 18, 38, 39, 69, 70
American Book Awards, 103

The American Cancer Society Cancer Book: Prevention, Detection, Diagnosis, Treatment, Rehabilitation, Cure, 83
American Civil Liberties Union, 72
American Diabetes Association, 87
American Institute of Architects, 97
American Journal of Alzheimer's Care and Related Disorders & Research, 45
American Library Association, 105–106
American Parkinson Association, 91
American Society on Aging, 13, 139
American Statistics Index, 28
Analytical Studies, 39
And the Home of the Brave, 111
Anderson-Ray, Susan M., 130
Andrus Gerontology Center, 65
Annual Review of Gerontology and Geriatrics, 29
Anthropology, 31, 137
Applewhite, Steven R., 119
Area Agencies on Aging, 25
Arthritis, 81–82, 86, 96, 142, 150
Arthritis: A Comprehensive Guide to Understanding Your Arthritis, 81, 82
Arthritis and the Elderly, 82
Arthritis Foundation, 81
The Arthritis Handbook: A Tested Self-Management Program for Coping with Your Arthritis, 82
Arthritis, Osteoporosis, Calcium and Estrogens, 19
Arthritis Relief at Your Fingertips: The Complete Self-Care Guide to Easing Aches and Pains without Drugs, 81
Asociación Nacional Pro Personas Mayores, 14
Assessing the Elderly: A Practical Guide to Measurement, 77
Association for Gerontology in Higher Education, 13, 26
Atchley, Robert, 29
Atkinson, Roland M., 40
Audio-Visual Resources for Gerontological and Geriatric Education, 17, 21
Averyt, Anne C., 128
Avioli, Louis V., 83

Baez, Joan, Senior, 151
Baker and Taylor, 12

Index

Balkema, John B., 21
Bangladesh, 36
Barresi, Charles M., 120
Bass, Scott, 122
Baulch, Evelyn M., 95
Be Well: The Later Years, 147–148
Beauvoir, Simone de, 29–30
Becerra, Rosina M., 119
Becker, Gaylene, 92–93
Behavior
    and aging, 4, 29, 30,
    and alcohol, 41
    problems in, 118
    research on, 37
Bereavement. *See* Grief
Berg, Kris E., 86
Bergstone, David, 26
Berle, Milton, 148
Bernstein, Joan B., 58
Bernstein, Merton C., 58
The Best of You, the Best of Me, 106
Best Wishes, Edith and Henry!, 111–112
Bibliographic Retrieval Services, 17
Bibliographies, 17, 21–22, 66–67, 73, 92, 105, 121, 149–150
Biermann, June, 87
Bi-Folkal Productions, 18
Billig, Nathan, 113–114
Binstock, Robert H., 30
Biology, 4, 24, 31, 38, 143
Biomedical research, 22, 29, 37, 38, 72
    in addiction, 42
    in Alzheimer's disease, 44
    in mental health, 115
Birren, James E., 68, 114
Black Adult Development and Aging, 120
Blacks, 14, 105, 120, 121, 132
Blindness. *See* Vision, loss of
Books in Print, 11
Borgatta, Edgar F., 134
Boston Women's Health Book Collective, 150
Botwinick, Jack, 30
Brandeis University, 123
Brecher, Edward M., 136
Brody, Stanley J., 74
Broomstick: By, for & about Women over Forty, 152
Brown, Robert N., 72

Brubaker, Timothy H., 102
Buchanan, Annette, 135
Bureau of National Affairs, 68
Burnside, Irene, 74, 114
Business, 23, 126
Butler, Robert N., 115, 136–137, 141

Calkins, E., 75
Callahan, Daniel, 72–73
Campbell, Scott, 53
Canada, 64, 97, 107
Cancer, 57, 83–84, 95, 96, 146
Cardiovascular health. *See* Heart disease
Care of elderly, 39, 76
    alternative, 53
    business aspects of, 47
    cost of, 50, 51
    by family, 47–53
    in home, 25–26, 29, 47–50, 96, 97, 107
    institutionalized, 21
    long-distance, 49
    nursing, 26–27
    personal, 25, 48, 96
    programs in, 52
    respite, 37, 108
    services for, 48–50, 52
    terminal, 23
    See also Daycare; Health care; Hospitals; Life care communities; Long-term care
Career Paths in the Field of Aging, 65
Caregivers, 4, 25, 42, 95–96, 129, 147, 150
    in Alzheimer's, 42–46, 117–118
    and chronic illness, 101
    emotional issues of, 48, 49, 51, 86
    in Parkinson's disease, 90, 91
    resources for, 51, 128
    in stroke, 85
    See also Care of elderly
Caregiving: Helping an Aging Loved One, 48
Caregiving with Grace, 45–46
Caring, 97
Caring for the Disabled Elderly: Who Will Pay?, 124
Caring for the Mentally Impaired Elderly: A Family Guide, 118

Caring for the Parkinson Patient: A Practical Guide, 90
Caring for Your Own: Nursing the Ill at Home, 96
Carlin, Vivian F., 98
Carter, Genevieve W., 130
Case Management and the Elderly: A Handbook for Planning and Administering Programs, 130
Case Western Reserve, 138
Cataracts, 93, 94
Cataracts: The Complete Guide—from Diagnosis to Recovery—for Patients and Families, 94
Chambré, Susan M., 125
Changes
 biological, 114
 life, 116, 151, 153
 physical, 78, 92, 144
 social, 33, 114, 144
Changing Health Care for an Aging Society: Planning for the Social Health Maintenance Organization, 123
Chapman, Elwood N., 47
Charles C Thomas, Publisher, 10
Chase, Deborah, 54
Cherlin, Andrew J., 102
Chernoff, Ronni, 141
Child, Julia, 151
Children, 103–106
Chinese language, 147
Choosing a Nursing Home: A Guidebook for Families, 109
Christensen, Alice, 141
Christianson, Jon B., 51
Church Council of Greater Seattle, 48
Churchill Films, 18
City of Green Benches: Growing Old in a New Downtown, 131
Clark, William F., 96
Classics in Aging, 100
Clearinghouse on Abuse and Neglect of the Elderly, 24
Clifford, Dennis, 54
Clinical Aspects of Aging, 77
Clinical Gerontologist: The Journal of Aging and Mental Health, 118–119
Close Harmony, 106–107

Coatesville-Jefferson conference, 40
Coberly, Lenore M., 125
Cohen, Donna, 115
Cohn, Keith, 84
Coleman, Barbara, 54
The Combined Problems of Alcoholism, Drug Addiction and Aging, 40
Comfort, Alex, 30, 138
Coming Back: A Guide to Recovering from Heart Attack, 84
The Coming of Age, 29
Commitment to an Aging Workforce: Strategies and Models for Helping Older Workers Achieve Full Potential, 68–69
Communication, 75–76, 117–118, 121, 129, 136
 devices for, 138–139
Communication Skills for Working with Elders, 75–76
Communications Technology and the Elderly: Issues and Forecasts, 138–139
Community services, 76, 127, 129–131
 in arthritis, 81
 in home care, 96–97
 in mental health, 115, 118
 in nutrition, 78, 80
 in therapy, 109
The Complete Book of Cancer Prevention: Foods, Lifestyles & Medical Care To Keep You Healthy, 83–84
The Complete Guide to Health Insurance: How To Beat the High Cost of Being Sick, 59
The Complete Guide to Living with High Blood Pressure, 85
Computer Technology and the Aged, 139–140
Computers, 139–140
Confused Minds, Burdened Families: Finding Help for People with Alzheimer's Disease and Other Dementias, 44
Congregate living, 25, 98–100
A Consumer Guide to Hospice Care, 54
Consumer Information Catalog, 19
Consumer Reports, 136
Consumers, 27, 33, 36, 39, 41
 and health, 142

Index

and long-term health care, 58
marketing to, 61
of senior services, 128
Consumer's Union, 136
Contemporary Long-Term Care, 110–111
Continuing care. *See* Life care
Cooney, Barbara, 103
Coping and Home Safety Tips for Caregivers of the Elderly, 101
Coping with Your Husband's Retirement, 133
Coronary Bypass Surgery: Who Needs It?, 84–85
Corporations, 27, 33
Counseling, 116, 117, 137
 See also Groups; Therapy
Counseling Elders and Their Families: Practical Techniques for Applied Gerontology, 116
Cowley, Malcolm, 31
Cox, Harold, 31
Coyle, Jean M., 149
Cozart, Carol, 150
The Crack-of-Dawn Walkers, 104
Creative Arts with Older Adults, 127
Creativity, 109–110, 125, 127
Crime, 4, 66–67, 128, 134, 135
Crime and the Elderly: An Annotated Bibliography, 66
Crow, Marjorie R., 75
Culture, 34, 122, 133
 See also Ethnicity
Cumulative Book Index, 9
Cunningham, Imogen, 27
Current Literature on Aging, 28
Current Population Reports, 36
Curtin, Sharon R., 31
Cusack, Odean, 75
Cutler, Winnifred B., 89

Dance, 109–110, 125–127
Data Resources in Gerontology: A Directory of Selected Information Vendors, 23
Databases, 23–24
Daubert, James R., 109
Daughters, 49–50, 150
 See also Families
Daughters of the Elderly: Building Partnerships in Caregiving, 49–50

Davis, P. J., 75
Daycare, 24, 48, 53, 108, 110, 128, 129, 132
 and Alzheimer's disease, 45
Death, 52, 56, 57, 80, 121, 128
 at home, 54
 of parents, 55
 of partner or spouse, 53–55, 117, 121
 preparing for, 78
 right to, 48, 57–58
 See also Hospice
De-institutionalization. *See* Institutionalization
Dementia, 43–45, 49, 101–102, 114, 118
 See also Alzheimer's disease
Demographics, 29, 32, 35, 51, 71, 119
 projections, 122, 123
Dennis, Helen, 69
Dentistry, 41
de Paola, Tomi A., 103
Dependency. *See* Independence
Depression, 85, 86, 113–114, 117
Design for Aging: An Architect's Guide, 97
Designing the Environment for Persons with Dementia, 101–102
Developing Adult Day Care: An Approach to Maintaining Independence for Impaired Older Persons, 128
Developments in Aging, 32
de Vries, Herbert A., 142
Diabetes, 86–87, 96, 137, 142, 146, 151
The Diabetic Woman, 87
Diabetic's Guide to Health and Fitness: An Authoritative Approach to Leading an Active Life, 86–87
Diagnosis Related Groups, 80
Dickinson, Peter A., 133
Diet and the Elderly, 19
Dippel, Raye L., 90
Directories, 10, 23–28, 111
Directory of Adult Day Care in America, 24
Directory of Nursing Homes, 24
Disabilities, 74, 79, 85, 92–94, 124
 and exercise, 147, 149
 and housing, 100
 and sexuality, 136
 and technology, 139, 140

Index

Displaced homemakers, 72
Distributors
 of books, 11–12, 105
 of films, 17–18
Diversity in Aging: Challenges Facing Planners and Policymakers in the 1990s, 122
Divorce, 102
Doing Things: A Guide to Programming Activities for Persons with Alzheimer's Disease and Related Disorders, 45
The Dollmaker, 52–53
Domestic Mistreatment of the Elderly—Towards Prevention, 66
Don't Take It Easy, 148
Doress, Paula Brown, 150
Douglass, Richard L., 66
Dreher, Barbara, 75
Drug abuse, 40–42
Drugs. *See* Medication
Drugs and the Elderly: Clinical, Social and Policy Perspectives, 41
Due upon Receipt, 63–64
Duke, Darby, 84
Duke University, 34
Dunkle, Ruth E., 84, 138
Duvoisin, Roger C., 90
Dychtwald, Ken, 32, 142
Dying at Home with Hospice, 54

Eastaugh, Steven R., 58
Easy Does It: Yoga for Older People, 141–142
Ebersole, Priscilla, 76
Economics, 21, 35, 37, 60–61, 123, 150
The Economics of Aging, 61
Edinberg, Mark A., 46
Education, 24, 33, 131, 145
 audiovisuals for, 21
 of elderly, 27, 35, 52, 65–66, 152
 films for, 22
 and technology, 139, 140
Educational Gerontology: An International Bimonthly Journal, 65
Eisdorfer, Carl, 115
Elder Abuse and Neglect: Causes, Diagnosis and Intervention Strategies, 67
Elder Cottage Housing Opportunities, 99
Elder Neglect and Abuse: An Annotated Bibliography, 66–67

Elderhostel, 29, 64
Elderhostel Catalog, 64
Elderhostels: The Students' Choice, 64
Elderly Patients and Their Doctors, 76–77
Elderly
 numbers of, 3, 5, 35, 47, 77, 108, 123, 124
 perceptions of, 32, 33
 photographs of, 31
 problems of, 29, 30, 32, 38
 as resources, 31–32
 treatment of, 31–32
Employee Benefit Research Institute, 62
Employment, 23, 33, 34, 68, 128, 150
 programs in, 68–69
 search for, 70, 152
 See also Work
Enabling the Elderly: Religious Institutions within the Community Service System, 130–131
The Encyclopedia of Aging, 22
Encyclopedia of Senior Citizens Information Sources, 23
Enjoying Old Age: A Program of Self-Management, 146
Environment and Aging, 100
Erikson, Erik, 32
Erikson, Joan, 32
The Essential Guide to Wills, Estates, Trusts and Death Taxes, 56
Estate planning, 54–56, 58, 73
Estes, Carroll L., 107, 122
Ethics, 132
 medical, 72–74, 77
Ethnic Dimensions of Aging, 120
Ethnicity, 26, 37, 119–122, 150
Ethnicity and Aging: A Bibliography, 121
Etten, Mary Jean, 78
Ettinger, Victor, 87
Euthanasia, 117
Exercise, 35, 48, 83, 114, 141–144, 146, 147, 149
 See also Fitness
Exercise Activities for the Elderly, 142, 143
Exercises for Non-Athletes over Fifty-One, 144
Exploding the Myths. Caregiving in America: A Study, 51

Index

Extended Health Care at Home: A Complete and Practical Guide, 95

Facilitating Education for Older Learners, 65
Failure-Free Activities for the Alzheimer's Patient: A Guidebook for Caregivers, 44
Falling, 79, 90
Falling in Old Age: Its Prevention and Treatment, 79
Families, 23, 34, 102, 128, 145, 150
   and chronic illness, 86
   communication in, 47, 108, 112
   and mental health, 116, 118
   See also Care of elderly; Caregiving
Family Caregiver's Guide: The Home Health Care Efficiency System that Really Works, 95–96
Family Relationships in Later Life, 102
Farber, Norma, 104
Federal policies. *See* Agencies; Policies
Fiction, 21–22, 103–106, 149
Fifty Plus, 40
Films, 22
Finances, 39, 40, 47, 48, 50, 52, 73, 145
   and business, 126
   in hospice, 54
   and parent's death, 55
   in retirement, 133–136
   and women, 150–153
   See also Investments
Finances after 50, 61
Financial planning, 58–59, 61, 64, 128, 135–136
Financing Health Care: Economic Efficiency and Equity, 58–59
Fisher, Lucy Rose, 150
Fisher, M. F. K., 151
Fitness, 39, 142, 144, 145, 148
   See also Exercise
Fitness after 50, 142
Fitness for the Aging Adult with Visual Impairment: An Exercise and Resource Manual, 145–146
Flatten, Kay, 142–143
Flowers, Joe, 32
Foehner, Charlotte, 150
Ford, A. B., 75

Forthcoming Books, 9
Foundations, 27
Fourteen Steps in Managing an Aging Work Force, 69
Fox, Mem, 104
Foyder, Joan Ellen, 95
Fraser, Virginia, 42
Fraud, 48, 108
French language, 75
Friedman, Jo-Ann, 96
Friedman, Roslyn, 133
Fries, James F., 81, 82
Funerals, 55
Furstenberg, Frank F., 102
Future, 29

Gach, Michael R., 81
The Gadget Book: Ingenious Devices for Easier Living, 139
Gallo, Joseph, 76
Gardening, 109, 127
Gays, 48, 121
Gelfand, Donald E., 119, 120, 128
Genetics, 114
George, Linda K., 30
Geriatric Drug Use—Chemical and Social Perspectives, 42
Geriatric Nutrition, 78
Geriatrics, 21, 25, 28, 29, 75, 79–80
   assessment in, 76, 77
   and drug abuse, 41
   education in, 26, 65–66
Geriatrics: For the Primary Care Physician, 79
Gerontological Association of America, 13
Gerontological Society of America, 37, 38
The Gerontologist, 37, 38
Gerontology, 23–25, 74, 121, 143
   applied, 115, 132, 144
   careers in, 65
   clinical, 118
   comparative, 26
   education in, 26, 65–66
   history of, 37
   literature on, 30
   psychosocial, 38, 77
   religious, 129, 132

Index

Gerontology (*continued*)
 research in, 26, 29, 31, 34, 38
 services in, 74, 129
 social, 21, 28
Gerontology & Geriatrics Education, 65–66
Geropsychological Assessment and Treatment: Selected Topics, 118
Get Up and Go, 91
Gifts of Age, 151
Gilford, Dorothy M., 123
Gillespie, Ann E., 98
Glaucoma, 23, 93
Gleason, Herbert L., 141
Going into Business for Yourself: New Beginnings after 50, 126
A Good Age, 30
Good Deeds in Old Age: Volunteering by the New Leisure Class, 125
Good Samaritan Hospital & Medical Center, 18
Gordon, Michael, 143
Gottheil, Edward, 40
Gourmet Recipes for Diabetics, 87
Government documents, 15–17, 23, 28
Government Printing Office, 16
Graebner, William, 133
Grambs, Jean D., 151
Grandpa Doesn't Know It's Me, 104
Grandparenthood, 102–105, 112, 151
Granny flats, 99
Grants, 23, 27–28, 37, 124
Gray Panther Network, 37
Gray Panthers, 33, 37
Great Britain, 36, 56
The Great Circle of Life: A Resource Guide to Films and Videos on Aging, 17, 22
Greenwood, Sadja, 90
Grief, 54–57, 103, 128
Group living. *See* Congregate living
Groups, 55, 114–115, 132, 138
 See also Counseling; Self-help; Therapy
Growing Old: A Handbook for You and Your Aging Parents, 51–52
Growing Old in Silence, 92
Growing Older, Getting Better: A Handbook for Women in the Second Half of Life, 151
Growing Wiser: The Older Person's Guide to Mental Wellness, 116

Growing Younger Handbook, 144
Guide to Health Insurance for People with Medicare, 20
A Guide to the Understanding of Alzheimer's Disease and Related Disorders, 43
Guthrie, Donna, 104
Gypsying after 40: A Guide to Adventure & Self-Discovery, 125

Hales, Dianne, 142
Handbook of Aging and the Social Sciences, 30
Handbook of Applied Gerontology, 144
Handbook of Geriatric Assessment, 76
Handbook of Gerontological Nursing, 78
Handbook of Gerontological Services, 129
Handbook of Mental Health and Aging, 114
Handbook of the Biology of Aging, 35
Handbook of the Psychology of Aging, 114
Harrington, Charlene, 107
Harris, Robert W., 125
Harvest Moon: Portrait of a Nursing Home, 110
Haug, Marie R., 76, 82, 138
Haworth Press, 10
Health, 4, 21, 23, 24, 27, 32, 34, 38–40, 128, 148, 150
 and aging, 47–49, 52, 116, 117
 assessment of, 78
 and life satisfaction, 38, 117
 promotion, 70, 141, 142, 147
 statistics on, 35, 39, 80
 and women, 150–152
 and work, 68
Health care, 21, 22, 38, 50, 108, 110, 134, 135, 145
 catastrophic, 62
 costs of, 49, 58–60, 62–63, 70–71, 123
 and drug abuse, 41, 42
 and employers, 70–71
 legal aspects of, 73
 perceptions about, 33
 research on, 29, 37
 resources, 72–73
 self-care, 50, 81, 141, 144, 150
 services for, 119, 128–130, 141–144
 and technology, 139, 140

Index

Health Care Financing Program Statistics, 60
Health Care Financing Review, 62–63
Health in the Later Years, 148
Health Insurance Association of America, 19
Health maintenance organizations, 50, 59, 97
Health Promotion and Disease Prevention in the Elderly, 141
Healthy Older People Program Memo, 147
Hearing loss, 92–93, 95, 138
Heart attack, 84–85
Heart Attack: What's Ahead?, 85
Heart disease, 84–86, 96, 146, 151
Heartland Journal, 127
Henig, Robin M., 42
Herr, John J., 116
Hess, Patricia, 76
Hessel, Dieter T., 33
Hest, Amy, 104
The Hidden Victims of Alzheimer's Disease: Families under Stress, 44–45
Highlights, 38
Hinrichsen, Gregory A., 116
HIP Report, 89
The Hispanic Elderly: A Research Reference Guide, 119
Hispanic Elderly in Transition, 119
Hispanics, 119
History, 18, 29, 30
A History of Retirement: The Meaning and Function of an American Institution, 133
Hobbies, 40, 143
Hochschild, Arlie R., 99
Hogue, Kathleen, 59
Home care. *See* Care of elderly
Home Health Care: A Complete Guide for Patients and Their Families, 96
Home safety, 20, 38, 101
  See also Crime
Home Safety Checklist for Older Consumers, 20
Homesharing and Other Lifestyle Options, 99
Hooyman, Nancy R., 47
Hormone therapy, 83, 89, 90, 137, 152

Horne, Jo, 48, 99
Horner, Catherine T., 105
Horticultural Therapy for Nursing Homes, Senior Centers, Retirement Living, 109
Hospice: Complete Care for the Terminally Ill, 56–57
The Hospice Journal: Psychological and Pastoral Care of the Dying, 57
The Hospice Movement: A Better Way of Caring for the Elderly, 56
Hospices, 25, 54, 56–57
Hospitals, 29, 39, 50, 59, 60
Hot Flash: A Newsletter for Midlife and Older Women, 152
Housing, 21, 23, 24, 32, 36, 40, 48, 49, 52, 128, 129, 145
  design of, 97–98, 100–102
  ownership of, 73
  public, 99
  research on, 37, 150, 151
  retirement, 133, 134
  and technology, 139, 140
Housing Interiors for the Disabled and Elderly, 100
Housing Options and Services for Older Adults, 98–99
Housing the Aged: Design Directives and Policy Considerations, 100
How Do I Pay for My Long-Term Health Care? A Consumer Guidebook about Long-Term Care Insurance, 58
How Does It Feel To Be Old?, 104
How To Hire Helpers: A Guide for Elders and Their Families, 48
How To Manage Older Workers, 69
How To Recruit Older Workers, 69
How To Treat Older Workers, 70
How To Use Private Health Insurance with Medicare, 19
Howells, John, 134
Humor, 145, 146
The Hundred Penny Box, 105
Huttman, Elizabeth D., 129
Hutton, J. Thomas, 90
Hygiene, 48
Hyman, Helen K., 50
Hyman, Mildred, 64
Hysterectomy, 89

I Know a Lady, 106
If I Live To Be 100: A Creative Housing Solution for Older People, 98
Illnesses
　catastrophic, 59
　chronic, 39, 82, 86, 118
　degenerative, 78, 86, 143
　of elderly, 50, 75
　prevention of, 141, 142, 146–147
　respiratory, 96
　and sexuality, 136, 137
　terminal, 56–58, 96
Income, 23, 32, 36, 59, 61, 73, 101, 116, 117
　support, 63, 64
Income of the Population 55 and Over, 59
Incontinence, 89
Independence, 25, 76, 117, 128, 129, 140, 141, 151–152
Index to Periodical Literature on Aging, 28
Indian Aging Agencies, 25
Informal Care of the Elderly, 51
Information Catalog for Partners in Health, 19
Inlander, Charles B., 59
Institute on Adult Day Care, 24
Institutionalization, 24, 79, 80, 117, 143
Insurance, 19, 26, 33, 135
　health, 58–62, 64, 152
　life, 61
　long-term care, 58, 124
　property, 61
　unemployment, 63
　See also Health maintenance organizations
An International Directory of Organizations in Aging, 24, 27
International Directory of Research and Researchers in Comparative Gerontology, 26
International Federation on Ageing, 36
The International Journal of Aging and Human Development: A Journal of Psychosocial Gerontology, 38
International Journal of Technology & Aging, 140–141
International research, 24, 35–36, 38, 150
Investments, 38, 61, 135

Is There No Place on Earth for Me?
Israel Levin Senior Adult Center, 122
It's Your Choice: The Practical Guide to Planning a Funeral, 55
Iverson, Laura, 70

Jarvik, Lissy F., 43, 48
Jensen, Cheryl, 59
Jews, 122
Job Search Manual for Mature Workers, 70
Job Training Partnership Act, 69
John Wiley and Sons, 11
Johnson, David R., 109
Johnson, Tanya F., 66
Jones, Reginald L., 120
Jorm, A., 43
Journal of Elder Abuse and Neglect, 67–68
Journal of Gerontological Social Work, 132
Journal of Gerontology, 38
The Journal of Minority Aging, 121
Journal of Nutrition for the Elderly, 80
Journal of Religion and Aging: The Interdisciplinary Journal of Practice, Theory, Applied Research, 132
Journals in Geriatrics and Gerontology: A Compendium for Authors, 25
Jovanovic, Lois, 87

Kalicki, Anne C., 26
Kamm, Phyllis, 56
Kane, Robert L., 77, 107, 108
Kane, Rosalie A., 77, 107, 108
Kapp, Marshall B., 73
Kapperud, Marla J., 93
Karr, Katherine, 108
Kart, Cary S., 143
Kastenbaum, Robert, 41
Katcher, Brian S., 88
Kate Quinton's Days, 130
Keep Movin': Fitness for Older Adults, 148–149
Keeping Out of Crime's Way: The Practical Guide for People over 50, 67
Kehoe, Monika, 120
Kemper, Donald W., 116, 144
Kingson, Eric R., 103
Kirnick, Helen, 32
Koehler, Barbara, 23
Koncelik, Joseph A., 99

Index

Kra, Siegfried, 84
Krames Communications, 19
Kuhn, Maggie, 33
Kushner, Irving, 81

La Buda, Dennis R., 139
Lammers, William W., 123
Later Life: The Realities of Aging, 31
Law, 27, 47–49, 51, 52, 128
  and business, 126
  and elder abuse, 66, 72
  and estates, 54, 56
  and guardianship, 118
  and health care, 73
  and hospices, 54
  and nursing homes, 108–109, 111
  and retirement, 134
  and widowhood, 150–151
Lawton, M. Powell, 100
Learning, 65, 114, 131
Learning To Live Well with Diabetes, 87
Lee, Philip R., 41
Le Fevre, Carol, 129
Le Fevre, Perry, 129
Legal and Ethical Aspects of Health Care for the Elderly, 73
Legal Aspects of Health Care for the Elderly: An Annotated Bibliography, 73
Legislation, 37–39
  See also Policies
Lerman, Liz, 125
Lesbians, 48, 120, 121
Lesbians over 60 Speak for Themselves, 120
Lesnoff-Caravaglia, Gari, 139, 144
Leutz, Walter N., 123
Lev, Yvonne, 23
Levin, Robert C., 70
Lewinsohn, Peter M., 118
Lewis, Myrna L., 115, 135–137
Lexington Books, 10
Ley, Olga, 144
Libraries, 7–9, 22, 131
Library Journal, 5
Lieberman, Abraham N., 91
Life care communities, 25–27, 98, 99
Life
  expectancy, 3, 35, 142
  extension of, 32, 72–73
  quality of, 39, 50, 73, 74, 133, 140
  satisfaction with, 38, 117, 132
Life magazine, 31
Lifestyles, 3, 27, 86, 133–135, 141, 149
Linked Lives: Adult Daughters and Their Mothers, 150
Linkletter, Art, 145
Lipschitz, David A., 141
Lipton, Helen L., 41
Literary Marketplace, 11
Literature, 22
  See also Fiction
Little, Billie, 87
Living arrangements, 52, 98–100, 130
  See also Congregate living; Housing; Retirement
Living wills, 49, 56, 57, 132
Living with Grace, 46
Lobenstine, Jay, 26
Loewinsohn, Ruth Jean, 54
Loneliness, 104, 116, 117, 145, 151–152
Longevity, 68, 141
Long-term care, 24, 36, 39, 51, 58–59, 77, 128, 129
  in Alzheimer's disease, 44, 95, 117–118
  benefits, 70–71, 107
  costs of, 62, 73, 108, 111, 118, 124
  facilities, 75, 96, 97, 110, 111
  at home, 95
  policies on, 107, 108, 110, 123, 124
  research in, 97, 107
  and technology, 140
  See also Nursing homes
Long-Term Care: Principles, Programs, and Policies, 108
Long-Term Care Demonstration, 51
Long-Term Care for the Elderly: A Factbook, 108–109
Long Term Care of the Elderly: Public Policy Issues, 107
Look Out for Annie, 94–95
Looking Forward: The Complete Medical Guide to Successful Aging, 146
Lorig, Kate, 82
Losing a Million Minds: Confronting the Tragedy of Alzheimer's Disease and Other Dementias, 44
Loss, 22, 35, 50, 116, 117
  See also Death

Index

Louis Harris and Associates, 33
Love and Sex after 40: A Guide for Men and Women for Their Mid and Later Years, 136
Love and Sex after 60, 136–137
Love, Sex, and Aging: A Consumer Union Report, 136
Lustbader, Wendy, 47

McClusky, Neil G., 134
Mace, Nancy L., 49
McGuire, Francis A., 139
MacLachlan, Patricia, 105
Maddox, George L., 22, 41
Maggie Kuhn on Aging, 33
Mahlmann, Diane E., 27
Mainstay: For the Well Spouse of the Chronically Ill, 86
Majors Scientific Books, 12
Managing Home Care for the Elderly: Lessons from Community-Based Agencies, 96–97
Mansberg, Ruth, 98
Marguia, Edward, 121
Marketing, 32, 59, 61, 110
Marketing Long-Term and Senior Care Services, 110
Marriage, 35, 102, 136, 137
and retirement, 133, 134
Maslow, Abraham, 76
Massow, Rosaline, 126
Mathis, Sharon B., 105
Matthews, Joseph L., 60
Matthews Books, 12
Mature Outlook, 38
Mayes, Kathleen, 82
The Measure of My Days, 35
Medicaid, 26, 58–60, 63, 107, 123, 124
Medical and Health Care Books and Serials in Print, 10, 11
Medical Ethics and the Elderly: A Case Book, 74
A Medical Handbook for Senior Citizens and Their Families, 146–147
Medical problems, 38, 52, 77, 136, 137
See also Health; Health care
Medicare, 26, 38, 59–63, 80
benefits, 60, 62, 63, 97, 123, 124
in hospice, 57
in long-term care, 58
Medicare and Medicaid Data Book, 60, 63
Medicare Made Easy, 59–60
Medication, 96, 147
and alcohol, 41
and dementia, 43
marketing of, 41
over-the-counter, 40, 42, 88–89, 146
for pain, 56
prescription, 62, 88–89, 98
and sexuality, 136, 137
side effects of, 49
testing of, 41
as therapy, 75, 78
Medicine, 24, 31
geriatric, 35, 41, 77
Medline, 24
Mellor, James W., 130
Memory loss, 49, 104, 114, 116, 150
Men, 123, 130
gay, 121
and sexuality, 136, 137
Mendleson, Mary A., 108
Menopause, 87, 89–90, 151
Menopause: A Guide for Women and the Men Who Love Them, 89–90
Menopause, Naturally: Preparing for the Second Half of Life, 90
Mental health, 41, 47, 49, 74, 97
maintaining, 144, 145, 148, 149
research on, 115, 118
resources for, 116
services for, 119
treatment of, 114–118
Mental Health Care of the Aging: A Multidisciplinary Curriculum for Professional Training, 115
Mental Health Problems and Older Adults, 116
Merrill, Fred L., 70
Metress, Seamus P., 143
Middle age, 4, 17, 32, 34, 150, 151
Middle Age and Aging: A Reader in Social Psychology, 34
Midlife and Older Women Book Project, 150
Miles Away and Still Caring: A Guide for Long-Distance Caregivers, 49
Miller, Alfred L., 93

Index

Miller, Mary, 117
Milletti, Mario A., 134
Minorities, 37, 102, 119–122
Mishara, Brian L., 41
Miss Rumphius, 103
Model Adult Protective Services Act, 67
Modern Maturity, 12, 39
Money. *See* Finances
Monk, Abraham, 129
Monthly Catalog of Government Publications, 15
Monthly Vital Statistics Report, 39
Moore, Steven R., 42
Morgan, Meredith W., 94
Mortality, 35, 39, 108
Moskowitz, Roland W., 82
Mourning. *See* Grief
Multiple sclerosis, 86
My Mother, My Father, 53
Myerhoff, Barbara, 122
Myers, Edward, 55
The Myth and Reality of Aging in America, 33
The Myth of Senility: The Truth about the Brain and Aging, 42–43

National Association for Families Caring for Their Elders, 14
National Association for Hispanic Elderly, 14
National Association for Home Care, 14
National Association for Parkinson's Disease, 90
National Association of Area Agencies on Aging, 14
National Caucus and Center on Black Aged, 14
National Center for Health Statistics, 39, 80
National Commission on Social Security Reform, 58
National Committee for the Prevention of Elder Abuse, 67
National Continuing Care Directory: Retirement Communities with Nursing Care, 26–27
National Council on the Aging, 13, 19, 24, 68, 132
National Directory of Educational Programs in Gerontology, 26
National Directory of Retirement Facilities, 25
National Gerontology Resource Center, 17
National Guide to Funding in Aging, 27–28
National Health and Nutrition Examination Survey, 39
National Hospice Organization, 57
National Hospital Discharge Survey, 80
National Indian Council on Aging, 14
National Institute for Mental Health, 16
National Institute on Adult Daycare, 132
National Institute on Aging, 16, 19, 37, 102
National Institute on Alcohol Abuse and Alcoholism, 41
National Institutes of Health, 19
National Interview Survey, 39
National Research Council, 123
National Senior Citizen's Law Center, 14
National Technical Information Service, 17
Native Americans, 14, 25, 121
Nature and Extent of Alcohol Problems among the Elderly, 41
Neglect. *See* Abuse
Neidrick, Darla J., 96
Nelson, Thomas C., 55
Neugarten, Bernice L., 34, 124
Neurochemistry, 35
Neurology, 57
The New American Grandparent: A Place in the Family, 102–103
New Choices for the Best Years, 40
Newman, Edwin, 72
1989–1990 Directory of State and Area Agencies on Aging, 25
1990 National Homecare and Hospice Directory, 25–26
Nobody Ever Died of Old Age, 31
Nonagenarians, 37
Normal Aging: Reports from the Duke Longitudinal Studies, 34
Norris, Jane, 49
Norway, 36
Notelovitz, Morris, 82
Now One Foot, Now the Other, 103–104

Number Our Days, 121–122
Nursing, 41, 57, 110
  geriatric, 75, 76, 78
  and mental health, 115
  research in, 74
Nursing and the Aged: A Self-Care Approach, 74
Nursing homes, 3, 24, 50, 52, 53, 104, 132
  abuses in, 108
  arts in, 127
  in Canada, 107
  choosing, 109
  costs of, 109
  health care in, 80, 108
  living in, 98, 109–113
  and Medicare, 60
  operation of, 110–111, 113
  regulation of, 108–109
Nursing Homes and Senior Citizen Care, 111
Nusberg, Charlotte, 26
Nussbaum, Annette, 133
Nutrition, 37, 38, 40, 41, 48, 80, 98, 141–144, 146–150
  and dementia, 43, 49
  and osteoporosis, 83
  programs in, 77–78, 128–129
Nutrition in the Later Years, 148
Nutrition, the Aged, and Society, 143–144

Oberg, Charles, 70
Octogenarians, 31–33, 35
Old age, 31, 35, 104
Old Age in the New Land, 29
Old Age Is Not for Sissies: Choices for Senior Americans, 145
Old Enough To Feel Better: A Medical Guide for Seniors, 143
Older Americans Act, 34, 122
Older Americans in the Workforce, 68
Older Americans Report, 124
Older Women's League, 15, 51
Olsen, Nancy, 126
On the Other Side of Easy Street: Myths and Facts about the Economics of Old Age, 60–61
Organizations, 24, 25, 27–28, 50
An Orientation to the Older Americans Act, 34

Orr, Nancy K., 44
Osgood, Nancy J., 117
Osteoporosis, 4, 82–83, 89, 90, 151
Osteoporosis: Brittle Bones and the Calcium Crisis, 82
Osteoporosis—The Silent Thief, 83
Ostroff, Jeff, 61
Ostrow, Andrew C., 145
Our Bodies, Ourselves, 150
Ourselves, Growing Older: Women Aging with Knowledge and Power, 150

Pacific Geriatric Education Center, 25
Painter, Charlotte, 151
Palder, Edward L., 135
Palmore, Erdman, 34
Parent Care: Resources To Assist Family Caregivers, 52
Parentcare: A Commonsense Guide for Adult Children, 48–49
Parents, care of, 47–50, 52–53
  See also Caregivers; Families
Parkinson's disease, 86, 90–91, 96, 142–143
Parkinson's Disease: A Guide for Patient and Family, 90
Parkinson's Disease Handbook: A Guidebook for Patients and Their Families, 91
Partners in Change, 71–72
Peale, Norman Vincent, 145
Peck, William A., 83
Peege, 112
Pelham, Anabel O., 96
Pensions, 3, 58, 60, 61, 134, 150
People's Medical Society, 59–60
Persico, J. E., 67
Peterson, David A., 26, 65
Pets, 75, 135
Pets and the Elderly, 75
Pharmacology for the Elderly: The Nurse's Guide to Quality Care, 75
Phillips, Alice H., 140
Photography, 31, 149
Physical Activity and the Older Adult: Psychological Perspectives, 145
Physical Change and Aging: A Guide for the Helping Professions, 78
Physical Fitness in the Later Years, 148

Index

Physicians, 50, 76–77, 79
Physician's Desk Reference, 88
Physician's Desk Reference for Nonprescription Drugs, 88–89
Physiology, 35, 138
Pitzele, Sefra Kobrin, 86
Plan Your Estate, 54
Planning Your Retirement Housing, 101
Polich, Cynthia L., 70
Policies
  on abuse, 68
  on Alzheimer's disease, 43, 44
  on caregiving, 51, 103
  on drugs, 41, 42
  federal, 23, 32, 34, 122, 124
  on health care, 123
  on housing, 100
  on long-term care, 107, 108, 110, 123, 124
  on mental health, 115
  on minorities, 120, 121
  on nursing homes, 109
  public, 107, 122–124
  on retirement, 134
  social, 29, 61, 122
  on Social Security, 63, 123
Porcino, Jane, 151
A Practical Guide to Hearing Aid Usage, 93
A Practical Guide to Independent Living for Older People, 140
The Practice of Geriatrics, 75
Prescription Drugs: An Indispensable Guide for People over 50, 88
Prevention magazine, 84
PRIDE Institute Journal of Long Term Home Health Care, 97
Prime Time: Sexual Health for Men over Fifty, 137
Product Directory and Buyers Guide, 111
Productive Aging: Enhancing Vitality in Later Life, 141
Products
  design of, 99–100, 139–141
  marketing of, 61, 111, 152
Programs, 22, 32, 38, 99, 124
  for care of elderly, 52, 131
  cost of, 61
  in employment, 68–69
  in nutrition, 77–78, 128–129

  planning, 130
  social, 131
Psychiatry, 31, 114, 118
Psychological problems, 52, 93, 94, 115, 118
  and caregiving, 96
  and sexuality, 136, 138
Psychology, 4, 22, 31
  of aging, 114, 116, 118
  of dying, 57
  and exercise, 145
  research in, 38, 114
  social, 34
Psychosocial issues, 29, 38, 77, 95, 150, 152
  and mental health, 115
  and substance abuse, 40
Public Policy and the Aging, 123
Publications, popular, 38–39
Publishers, 9–11, 17, 27
Publishers, Distributors, and Wholesalers of the United States, 11
Publisher's Trade List Annual, 9
Publishers Weekly, 9
Pulitzer Prize, 130
Purcell, Julia, 85
Pynoos, Jon, 100

Q and A: Alzheimer's Disease, 19
Quiet Fire: Memoirs of Older Gay Men, 121
Quinn, Mary J., 67

Rabin, David L., 108
Rabins, Peter V., 49
Radio Shack, 19
Rainbow Series, 39
Ralston, Jeannie, 145
Rankin, David, 141
Raper, Ann Trueblood, 26
Raschko, Bettyann B., 100
Reader's Digest, 40
Reagan, Nancy, 145
Reagan, Ronald, 145
Recreation, 21, 52, 125–127, 139, 142, 143
Recreation Activities for the Elderly, 142, 143
Rees, Michael K., 85

Regan, John L., 73
Regnier, Victor, 100
Rehabilitation, 74, 92
Reichel, William, 77
Relationships, 22, 48, 121, 137, 138, 149, 150, 153
  intergenerational, 61, 102–107
  See also Families
Religion, 33, 129–132, 150
Resource Directory for Older People, 27
A Resource Guide for Nutrition Management Programs for Older Persons, 77–78
Resource Guide of Continence Products and Services, 89
Resources To Go, 18
Retirement, 3, 23, 128, 151
  adjusting to, 133, 134
  attitudes toward, 33, 34
  benefits in, 70
  communities, 26–27, 110, 124, 135
  costs of, 101, 133–135
  early, 68, 71
  facilities for, 25
  history of, 133
  housing in, 101
  income in, 32, 61
  in Japan, 36
  planning, 61, 68, 101, 133–136, 148
  policies on, 134
  resources on, 135
  and Social Security, 58
  of spouse, 133
The Retirement Account Calculator: Complete Savings and Withdrawal Tables for IRA and Keogh Plans, 135
Retirement Choices: For the Time of Your Life, 134
Retirement Edens outside the Sunbelt, 133
The Retirement Sourcebook: Your Complete Guide to Health, Leisure, and Consumer Information, 135
Reyes-Watson, Eleanor, 142–143
Rheumatism, 81
Richard, Marty, 109
The Right To Die . . . The Choice Is Yours, 57–58
Rights, 57–58, 60, 72–73
The Rights of Older Persons, 72

Rivlin, Alice M., 124
The Road Ahead: A Stroke Recovery Guide, 85
Robinson, Anne, 117
Roe, Daphne A., 78
Role theory, 35
Roman, Caryl K., 140
Rosenberg, Marvin, 138
Rosenbloom, Alfred A., 94
Rosow, Irving, 34–35
Ross, Mary Alice, 145
Rossman, Isadore, 146
Rothert, Eugene A., 109
Rowe, John W., 35
R. R. Bowker, 11, 131
Rubenstein, Robert L., 130
Ruff, George E., 74
Ruth Stout's Garden, 127

Safford, Florence, 118
St. Petersburg, Florida, 131
Sandel, Susan L., 109
Saxon, Sue V., 78
Schaie, K. Warner, 114
Schick, Frank L., 22
Schmidley, James W., 84
Schneider, Edward L., 35
Schover, Leslie R., 137
Schultz, James H., 61
Scott-Maxwell, Florida, 35
The Search for Intimacy: Love, Sex and Relationships in the Later Years, 138
Sears, Roebuck and Co., 20, 38
Sears Specialog: Home Health Care, 20
Selden, Ira Lee, 126
Selected Products for People with Special Needs, 19
Self-help, 27, 53, 55, 115, 137, 143
Senility, 42–43
  See also Alzheimer's disease
Senior centers, 107, 130, 132
Senior citizens. *See* Elderly
Seniors Medication Education Program, 20
Sensory change, 92, 141, 146
  See also Hearing loss; Vision
Services, 22, 32, 34, 38, 128–132, 152
  for Alzheimer's disease, 42, 44
  for care of elderly, 48, 49, 50, 52, 110

geriatric, 74
gerontological, 129
health, 119
for mental health, 116, 119
in retirement, 133
social, 27, 35, 36, 38, 115, 119, 129
See also Community services
Serving the Older Adult: A Guide to Library Programs and Information Services, 131
Seskin, Jane, 151
Setting Limits, 72–73
Seven Days a Week, 112–113
Sex after 60, 136
Sexuality, 48, 89, 114, 118, 136–138, 150–152
Sexuality in the Later Years: Roles and Behavior, 137–138
Shane, Dorlene V., 61
Sheehan, Susan, 130
Shelley, Florence D., 50
Sheridan, Carmel, 44
Sherman, Michael, 135
Shields, Laurie, 50
Shulman, Julius, 94
Silverman, Phyllis R., 53, 55
Silverstone, Barbara, 50
Singles, 134, 152
Singular Paths: Old Men Living Alone, 130
Skinner, B. F., 146
Sleep, 29
Sloan, Katrinka Smith, 98
Sloane, R. Bruce, 114
Small, Gary, 48
Smith, Elaine, 75
Social Forces and Aging: An Introduction to Social Gerontology, 29
Social issues, 22, 23, 29, 34, 61, 94, 114, 120, 122, 134, 136, 143, 144
See also Psychosocial issues
Social sciences, 24, 30, 31, 37, 38, 41, 42
Social SciSearch, 24
Social Security, 33, 37, 58, 61–62, 133
benefits, 60, 62, 134
policy on, 123
Social Security: The System That Works, 58
Social Security Administration, 16, 62, 63
Social Security Bulletin, 63
Social Security Bulletin Annual Statistical Supplement, 63
Social Security Handbook, 62
Social Security Manual, 61–62
Social Security, Medicare and Pensions: A Sourcebook for Older Americans, 60
Social Services for the Elderly, 129
Social work, 31, 115, 132
Socialization, 34–35
Socialization to Old Age, 34
Sociology, 4, 31, 35, 138
Sokolovsky, Jay, 26
Soled, Alex J., 56
Sommers, Tish, 50
Spanish language, 14, 36, 119, 147
A Special Trade, 105–106
Spencer, Beth, 117
Sports, 38
Springer Publishing Co., 10
SRx, 20
Stand Tall! The Informed Woman's Guide to Preventing Osteoporosis, 82–83
Stanford University Arthritis Clinic, 81–82
Starr, Bernard D., 137
The Starr-Weiner Report on Sex and Sexuality in the Mature Years, 137
Starting a Mini-Business: A Guidebook for Seniors and Others Who Dream of Having Their Own Part-Time, Home-Based Business, 126
Statistical Handbook on Aging Americans, 22
Statistical Reference Index, 28
Statistics, 22–23, 28
health, 39, 80
international, 35–36
population, 36
vital, 39, 80
Staying Active: Wellness after Sixty, 149
Steffl, Bernita M., 78
Steinberg, Raymond M., 130
Stephens, Susan A., 51
Stereotypes, 30, 31, 33, 34, 131, 141, 143, 153
and benefits, 124
economic, 60
and sexuality, 137–138, 151
and work, 69, 71, 72, 151
Stockton, Patricia, 108

Stoddard, Sandol, 56
Stone, Robyn, 51
Stress
　and cardiovascular diseases, 84
　of caregivers, 44–45
　management of, 142, 149
　and mental health, 117
　and sexuality, 136
　and work, 68
Stress in the Later Years, 148
Stroke, 84–86, 146
Stroke in the Elderly: New Issues in Diagnosis, Treatment and Rehabilitation, 84
Strong, Maggie, 86
Stroud, Marion, 79
Substance abuse, 40, 116
　See also Alcoholism; Drug abuse
Successful Aging: A Sourcebook for Older People and Their Families, 128
Successful Marketing to the 50+ Consumer, 61
Suicide, 117
Suicide after Sixty: The Final Alternative, 117
Suicide in the Elderly: A Practitioner's Guide to Diagnosis and Mental Health Intervention, 117
Sumichrast, Michael, 101
Sunderland, George, 67
Survival Handbook for Widows (and for Relatives and Friends Who Want To Understand), 54–55
Sutton, Evelyn, 79

Taking Care: Supporting Older People and Their Families, 47–48
Talking with Your Aging Parents, 47
Taxes
　in business, 126
　estate, 56, 150
　income, 73
　property, 101
　sales, 101
Taylor, George A., 74
Teacher's Insurance and Annuity Association, 134–135
Teaching Dance to Senior Adults, 125–126

Technology, 138–141
Technology and Aging in America, 140
Teel, Thomas W., 42
Tender Loving Greed: How the Incredibly Lucrative Nursing Home Industry Is Exploiting America's Old People and Defrauding Us All, 108
Teri, Linda, 118
Terra Nova Films, 18
Therapy
　art, 127
　dance, 109–110, 127
　drama, 109–110, 127
　hormone replacement, 83, 89, 90, 137, 152
　horticultural, 109
　mental health, 115
　music, 115, 127
　poetry, 118
　writing, 127
Third World, 78
The 36-Hour Day: A Family Guide to Caring for Persons with Alzheimer's Disease, Related Dementing Illness, and Memory Loss in Later Life, 49
Thomas, William W., 61
Thornton, Howard A., 146
Thornton, Susan M., 42
Thrifty Meals for Two, 19
Through Grandpa's Eyes, 105
Tideiksaar, Rein, 79
Ties that Bind: The Interdependence of Generations, 103
Tisdale, Sallie, 110
To Be Old and Sad: Understanding Depression in the Elderly, 113–114
Tobin, Sheldon S., 130
Tomb, David A., 51
Tomita, Susan K., 67
Toohey, Barbara, 87
Toward Healthy Aging: Human Needs and Nursing Responses, 76
Transportation, 128, 129
Travel, 38–40, 125, 126, 133
Travel Easy: The Practical Guide for People over 50, 126
Treatments for the Alzheimer Patient: The Long Haul, 43
Trieschmann, Roberta B., 92

Index

Turock, Betty J., 131
The Two of Them, 103

Ulrich's International Periodicals Directory, 10
Understanding Arthritis, 81
Understanding Difficult Behaviors: Some Practical Suggestions for Coping with Alzheimer's Disease and Related Illnesses, 117
Understanding "Senility": A Layperson's Guide, 42
Unemployment, 133
The Unexpected Community: Portrait of an Old Age Subculture, 99
The Unfinished Business of Living: Helping Aging Parents Help Themselves, 47
United Seniors Health Cooperative, 61
University of California–Berkeley, 32–33
University of Southern California, 26
Urban, Kathleen M., 59
Urban renewal, 131
U.S. Bureau of the Census, 3, 35, 36, 37
U.S. Congress, Office of Technology Assessment, 44, 140
U.S. Consumer Product Safety Commission, 20
U.S. Department of Health and Human Services, 62
U.S. Directory and Source Book on Aging, 27
U.S. Food and Drug Administration, 41
U.S. Health Care Financing Administration, 20, 37, 62
U.S. House Select Committee on Aging, 15
U.S. Senate Special Committee on Aging, 16, 23, 32

Vacha, Keith, 121
Vaughan, Margaret E., 146
Venice, California, 122
Vesperi, Maria D., 131
Veterans, 60, 63
Veterans Administration, 60
The View from Eighty, 31
Vision, 92–95, 106, 138, 145–146
Vision and Aging: General and Clinical Perspectives, 94

Vital and Health Statistics, 39
Vital and Health Statistics Series, 80
Vital Involvements in Old Age, 32
Voices of Experience: 1500 Retired People Talk about Retirement, 134–135
Volunteers, 23, 115, 125, 128, 132, 135, 141
Von Behren, Ruth, 132

Waiting at the Gate: Creativity and Hope in the Nursing Home, 109–110
Walking, 145
Walking for the Health of It: The Easy and Effective Exercise for People over 50, 145
Ware, Marsha, 82
Wasserman, Paul, 23
Waymack, Mark H., 74
W. B. Saunders, 10
We Are Not Alone: Learning To Live with Chronic Illness, 86
Weakland, John H., 116
Weaver, Peter, 135
Weg, Ruth B., 137
Weiner, Marcella Baker, 137
Weisberg, Naida, 127
Weiss, David M., 27
Weizman, Savine G., 56
Wellness, 70, 116, 142, 149
Wellness and Health Promotion for the Elderly, 142
Wellness Programs for Older Workers and Retirees, 70
Wesley Hall: A Special Life, 113
What Do I Do? How To Care for, Comfort and Commune with Your Nursing Home Elder, 108
What To Do with What You've Got: The Practical Guide to Money Management in Retirement, 135–136
When Hearing Fades: Perspectives on Hearing Loss in Later Years, 95
When Parents Die: A Guide for Adults, 55
When Your Parents Grow Old, 50
Where Can Mom Live? A Family Guide to Living Arrangements for Elderly Parents, 98
Where Coverage Ends: Catastrophic Illness and Long-Term Health Care Costs, 62

White, Laurie, 117
Who Will Pay? The Employer's Role in Financing Health Care for the Elderly, 70–71
Widower, 53
Widowhood, 53–55, 130, 150–151
The Widow's Handbook: A Guide for Living, 150–151
Widow-to-Widow, 55
Wiener, Joshua M., 124
Wilder, Rosilyn, 127
Wilfred Gordon McDonald Partridge, 104
Wilhite, Barbara, 142–143
A Will and a Way: What the United States Can Learn from Canada about Caring for the Elderly, 107
William, J. Winston, 110
Wills, 54, 56, 73
Winograd, Carol H., 43
Wittman, Sally, 105
Wolfe, Sidney M., 89
Women, 3, 33, 121, 123, 149–153
    as caregivers, 50–51
    and diabetes, 87
    and employment, 72, 151
    in midlife, 150–151
    and osteoporosis, 82–83
    and sexuality, 136, 137, 150–152
    See also Menopause; Widows
Women and Aging: A Selected Annotated Bibliography, 149–150
Women and Aging: An Anthology by Women, 149

Women over 40, 151
Women Take Care: The Consequences of Caregiving in Today's Society, 50–51
Work, 48, 140, 151
Workers, 4, 38, 69–71
Workers over 50: Old Myths, New Realities, 71
Workforce, aging, 68, 69, 71
Working Age, 71
Working with the Elderly: Group Process and Techniques, 114–115
Worst Pills, Best Pills: The Older Adult's Guide to Avoiding Drug-Induced Death or Illness, 89
Writers Have No Age: Creative Writing with Older Adults, 125
Writing, 125, 127, 149

Yahnke, Robert, 17, 22
Yankelovich, Skelly, and White, 71
Yoga, 141–142
Yolles, Stanley, 71
You and Your Aging Parent: The Modern Family's Guide to Emotional, Physical, and Financial Problems, 50
Your Legal Rights in Later Life, 73

Zarit, Judy M., 44
Zarit, Steven H., 44
Zgola, Jitka M., 45
Zimmerman, Jack M., 56
Zolotow, Charlotte, 106

NO LONGER THE PROPERTY
OF THE
UNIVERSITY OF R.I. LIBRARY